# MARRIA

A Manual for Refreshing Marriages with Principles from God's Word. For Pre-married Couples, and those whose Marriages have Lasted These Many Years

by

**Paul Frederick**

with

**Maurice Russell**

*To my FRIENDS, Jim + ANN-MARIE*

*Maurice Russell*

*THANKS FOR EVERYTHING*

*Printed in the United States of America*
*2018*

**TABLE OF CONTENTS**

**BOOK ONE – PRE-MARRIAGE COUNSELING**

3

## BOOK TWO
## REFRESHER FOR HUSBANDS, REFRESHER FOR WIVES

PREMARRIAGE SESSIONS

## APPENDICES

## INTRODUCTION:

"Pastor, I'd like to learn how you do pre-marriage counseling for young couples." I was a young pastoral intern riding to a meeting with my pastor-mentor, Rev. Paul Frederick.

"Do you have a pen and paper?" Pastor Frederick asked as he drove. Over the next forty or fifty minutes he gave me his pre-marriage counseling outline, with insightful explanations. I copied as fast as I could.

Throughout my thirty-five years in ministry I have used Pastor Frederick's notes to shape my pre-marriage counseling ministry with more than fifty couples.

I suggested to Pastor Frederick that we put his pre-marriage counseling notes and mine together into a book. I thought these notes would help young pastors seeking to biblically counsel young couples in preparation for their marriages, and they might refresh any marriage by application of these biblical teachings.

Pastor Frederick agreed.

Here it is.

"Book 1," is designed for pre-marriage counseling. "Book 2," beginning on page 83, adapts these biblical teachings for the refreshment of all husbands and wives.

# BOOK 1 - PRE-MARRIAGE COUNSELING

## THE INTRODUCTORY MEETING

As a pastor you never know when you will be asked to conduct a funeral or officiate a wedding. In most cases neither event is in your annual plan.

When the call comes that a couple would like to get married, before you give them an answer, it is a good idea to schedule an introductory meeting. Even if you know the couple well, this introductory meeting and their answers to these questions may prove valuable to you as their pastor. What you learn may shape future counseling sessions with them.

I have prepared an interview sheet you can print. You can use the sheet and fill in the answers as you ask the questions orally.

If on occasion you have to do pre-marriage counseling remotely and you can email these introductory sheets to the prospective bride and groom to fill out and email back to you.

In any event, this interview will give you insight into their spiritual commitment, their maturity, and their understanding of marriage and how their marriage relates to their families.

The notes you jot down on this questionnaire sheet provide you with valuable contact information and dates for your records.

## PRE-MARRIAGE "GETTING ACQUAINTED" MEETING WITH AN INTERESTED COUPLE

NAMES:          (John E. Jones)          (Mary K. Mouse)

AGES:           21                       22

ADDRESSES:

PHONES:

OCCUPATIONS:

    How long have you worked there?

    Do you like it?

    Plan to stick with it?

EDUCATION:

    Where?

    What degree?

    Do you anticipate more schooling?

HOMETOWNS?

SIZE OF YOUR FAMILIES?

HOW LONG HAVE YOU KNOWN EACH OTHER?

HOW DID YOU MEET?

HOW LONG HAVE YOU DATED EACH OTHER?

EITHER BEEN MARRIED BEFORE? (If Yes, discuss the matter)

DATE YOU WOULD LIKE TO BE MARRIED?

WHERE ARE YOU IN YOUR SPIRITUAL JOURNEY?
(Gospel track - What do these verses say to you?)
Rom. 3:23
Rom. 6:23
John 14:6
1 Corinthians 15:3 - Why did Jesus die on the cross?
John 1:12
1 John 1:9
Rom. 10:9

WHY ARE YOU COMING TO A PASTOR RATHER THAN JUSTICE OF PEACE?
> (Why is church important?)
> - Establish the importance to God of marriage.
> - Ephesians 5:22-33 Marriage is part of much greater picture.

COMMON INTERESTS? HOBBIES?

DESCRIBE YOUR FIANCEE FOR ME:
> Interests     Values
> Strengths     Areas that need work

DO YOU KNOW ONE ANOTHERS' FAMILIES?

DO YOU LIKE THEM?

DO THEY LIKE YOU?

DO YOU KNOW ONE ANOTHERS' FRIENDS?

DO YOU LIKE THEM?

WHAT DO YOUR PARENTS THINK OF YOUR PLANS?

ARE YOU LIVING TOGETHER? SLEEPING TOGETHER?
ENGAGING IN SEXUAL RELATIONS?

Note: If the couple is engaging in sexual relations, it is important that they are reminded of what God's Word says about that behavior. They need to confess their sin and repent—turn away—quit having sexual relations until after they are married.

It may be at this time that the pastor has opportunity to lead one or both the man and the woman to faith in Jesus Christ.

If the couple is living together, I offer them two options:

1. Separate and move apart until after the wedding—making a commitment to refrain from sex until after the wedding. One or both of them may be able to move back home to parents, or to rent a place for a short time.

2. If they cannot figure a way to move apart, then the second option is to have a private wedding as soon as possible—within days—and then plan the formal, public celebration of their marriage later.

In either case, the pastor still needs to counsel the couple to confess their sin and refrain from sex until after their marriage.

IF THEY ARE SLEEPING TOGETHER AND DON'T SEE
WHAT'S WRONG WITH THAT, here is some Scripture to
help to lead the couple in a discussion of God's Plan and
how they can fit into His Plan.:

Do you know what God expects of those who trust in
Christ?

**1 Corinthians 6:18-7:2 (NIV)**

*Flee from sexual immorality. All other sins a man commits
are outside his body, but he who sins sexually sins against
his own body. [19]Do you not know that your body is a temple
of the Holy Spirit, who is in you, whom you have received
from God? You are not your own; [20]you were bought at a
price. Therefore honor God with your body.*

*[7:1]Now for the matters you wrote about: It is good for a
man not to marry. [2]But since there is so much immorality,
each man should have his own wife, and each woman her
own husband.*

**1 Thes. 4:3-8 (NIV)**

*It is God's will that you should be sanctified: that you
should avoid sexual immorality; [4]that each of you should
learn to control his own body in a way that is holy and
honorable, [5]not in passionate lust like the heathen, who do
not know God; [6]and that in this matter no one should wrong
his brother or take advantage of him. The Lord will punish
men for all such sins, as we have already told you and*

*warned you.* ⁷*For God did not call us to be impure, but to live a holy life.* ⁸*Therefore, he who rejects this instruction does not reject man but God, who gives you his Holy Spirit.*


ASK your couple: What is your response to what God expects, as He has stated in these passages?

My next step is to explain what kind of PREMARRIAGE
COUNSELING I do:

1. I tell the couple that I do *biblical* pre-marriage
   counseling. That means that everything that I
   share with a pre-marriage couple is drawn from
   God's Word. I try not to *make up* anything about
   marriage that is extra-biblical.

   BIBLICAL COUNSELING, unlike the advice
   commonly available, asks:
   - What does God's Word say?
   - What does it say to me?
   - What am I going to do about it?

   I tell the couple that I don't do
   "psychological" counseling. If they need that,
   they will have to look for it somewhere else.

2. You may find the video series, "MAXIMUM
   MARRIAGE" by Pastor Tommy Nelson, to be
   especially helpful and enjoyable to view. At the
   end of each session you could send a few of the
   videos with the couple for them to watch
   together.

3. It has been my practice as a pastor when I am
   counseling a couple, to require them to weekly
   attend the church where I am serving during our
   counseling sessions and until they are married.

4. If your church has Wedding Policy guidelines,
   provide a copy to the couple, reading to them
   any part that seems especially noteworthy.

5.  If your church has a Fee Agreement Sheet, ask the couple to go over it together, agree to it, sign the agreement and return it to you.

6.  If your church uses a Wedding Coordinator, introduce them to the Wedding Coordinator. She (or he) will help them plan their wedding. Under the direction of the pastor, the Coordinator will assist in conducting the wedding party through the ceremony.

7.  Explain to the couple the importance of their keeping timely appointments to meet with you for a series of general pre-marriage and financial counseling sessions. (Some states have substantial discounts off the wedding license fee for couples who take a number of hours—12 hours in Minnesota—of pre-marriage counseling. Check with your county clerk.)

**PREMARRIAGE SESSIONS**

I usually plan two hours for each meeting with the pre-marriage couple. During that time, I cover one or two sessions with them. After the above introductory material, start with:

**SESSION 1: FOUNDATION FOR A LIFE-LONG CHRISTIAN MARRIAGE:**

A life-long Christian marriage begins with **Faith in Jesus Christ as your personal Savior.** (Some couples or individuals may need further teaching about what it means to trust Jesus as Savior. This is a good place for that.)

A life-long Christian marriage requires **Mutual Commitment.** **Ephesians 4:25** *Therefore, putting away lying, "Let each one of you speak truth with his neighbor," for we are members of one another.* All your life, **Be Honest with God.** All your life, **Be Honest with each other.**

A life-long Christian marriage needs **Good Communication.**

Three Common barriers to good communication:

a. Problems with Anger (Ephesians 4:26-31)

b. Problems with sex (Ephesians 5:25-28)

c. Problems with money (Proverbs 13:7)

(Promise the couple, "We will talk about all three of these problems in our counseling sessions together.")

## SCRIPTURAL BACKGROUND FOR MARRIAGE

**Ephesians 5:31-33** - Why marriage is so important:

These verses show us that God's intention is to paint marriage as a picture of the right, loving relationship between Christ and His Church.

- The Man is to care for, and love, his wife sacrificially, as Christ cares for and loves His Bride, the Church.

- The Woman is called to lovingly respond to her husband, just as the Church (the body of believers who love and trust the Lord Jesus) responds with faithful love for Christ.

Marriage involves submission to each other.

**Ephesians 5:21** *submitting to one another in the fear of God.*

"Submission" – Is this a positive or a negative word?

The beauty of "submission" and "authority" is shown to us in the Bible through the relationship between God as Father and as Son.

**Philippians 2:5-11** *Let this mind be in you which was also in Christ Jesus,* (**the Son**) *⁶ who, being in the form of God, did not consider it robbery to be equal with God,* (**the Father**) *⁷ but made Himself of no reputation,* (**the Son submitted to the Father by**) *taking the form of a bondservant, and coming in the likeness of men. ⁸ And being found in appearance as a man, He humbled Himself and*

17

*became obedient to the point of death, even the death of the cross. ⁹ Therefore God also has highly exalted Him and given Him the name which is above every name, ¹⁰ that at the name of Jesus every knee should bow, of those in heaven, and of those on earth, and of those under the earth, ¹¹ and that every tongue should confess that Jesus Christ is Lord, to the glory of God the Father.*

Submission means that marriage is not a fifty-fifty relationship, but both husband and wife give themselves 100% to each another as long as they both shall live. The character quality of *selflessness* is essential in a Christian marriage:

- Giving up selfish expectations.
- Submission means identifying your God-given role (as husband or as wife) and fitting into that role biblically.
- Submission means serving each other, not demanding service from one another.
- It means disposing of non-Biblical attitudes and ideas.

ASK your couple: "Where might non-Biblical attitudes and ideas come from?"

Listen for their insights as each of them thinks through the question—maybe even have them discuss it between themselves.

Eventually, the pastor may want to add his own thoughts, that non-Biblical attitudes can come from TV, internet, well-meaning friends, school, and even our own inner thoughts.

But wherever non-biblical attitudes and ideas come from, if brought into the marriage circle, they will corrode the marriage bond. Without realizing that we are doing so, it is easy to adopt non-biblical attitudes, words, phrases and jokes that we hear around us. Encourage wise discernment in the attitudes and ideas your couple adopts as their own.

Well-meaning friends who are not familiar with their Bibles can give damaging, non-biblical counsel to us.

A few **practices to intentionally avoid** include:

- talking in negative ways *to* your spouse or talking *about* your spouse to other people;

- making jokes or telling embarrassing stories about your spouse unless you have express permission to "tell that story."

God's design for marriage involves a husband and a wife who will practice **sacred respect and honor** toward each another.

**Let's talk about Teamwork in your marriage:**

**Work** at understanding each other. It is easy to misunderstand each other. Understanding one another takes determined effort.

**AVOID:**

1) Discussing with friends or family members any marriage problems between you and your spouse
2) phrases such as: "What's that supposed to mean?"

**THINK:**

1) the best of each other
2) the best of one another's intentions and motives

**WHAT IS LOVE?** (as defined in God' Word)

Have your couple open their Bibles to 1 Corinthians 13:4-8. Before you read this passage to your couple, say, "Watch for anything that seems different in this passage about love from the way that we normally think about love?"

READ:

**1 Corinthians 13:4-8**

*Love suffers long and is kind; love does not envy; love does not parade itself, is not puffed up;*
*5 does not behave rudely, does not seek its own, is not provoked, thinks no evil;*
*6 does not rejoice in iniquity, but rejoices in the truth;*
*7 bears all things, believes all things, hopes all things, endures all things.*
*8 Love never fails. . .*

ASK: Did you notice anything about God's description of love that is different from the way we think of love, or the way we sing about it in popular music?

Wait while they think and maybe give an answer (or maybe not).

Pastor: "God's idea of love does not deal directly with emotions like our ideas often do. This passage tells us that *love is active.* All of these phrases are action phrases."

**1 Corinthians 13:4-8a (NIV)**

1. Be patient,
2. Be kind.
3. Do not envy,
4. Do not boast,
5. Don't be proud
6. Don't be rude,
7. Don't insist on your own way,
8. Don't be irritable (or irritating),
9. Keep no record of wrongs
10. Do not delight in evil (or when evil-doers meet God's justice – Psalm 73:1-22)
11. Rejoice when the Truth wins out
12. Protect, *to roof over; to cover with silence* – (Strong's Concordance)
13. Always respect
14. Always expect the best
15. Always persevere.
16. Never quit, nor give up. (v. 8a)

This is the character and behavior of God-given love—what love *is* and what love *does*. Love acts this way. That's why we can keep our marriage vows. Even if we are upset with each other, we can love—we can behave as God tells us to in this passage.

Married couples would do well to print this list and put it on their refrigerator. Each morning they should ask the Lord to help them love as God tells us to love in this passage of His Word. At the end of each day they could go down the list, evaluating how they have done. "Did this well. Did this well. Oops, not so good here. I need to work on this one. Etc."

A husband or a wife could do this all their lives and continually grow in Christ-like love.

End this session with these few words of wisdom for building good marriage relations together.

1. Always be trustworthy. Keep your word. Keep appointments.

    Keep your promises.

2. Trust each another.

3. Your love must be tough.

    Difficult times will come.

    When then do, work together.

    Help each other.

    Comfort one another.

(For personal study of submission, the pastor might want to consider the studies in Appendices #3 and #4.)

**SESSION 2: FOUNDATIONAL LOVES FOR A CHRISTIAN MARRIAGE**

Here are some verses to use in helping your couple realize what it means to have a fully rounded love-life as designed for us by the Lord Himself.

**1. Love the Lord - Matthew 22:37-38** *Jesus said to him, "'You shall love the LORD your God with all your heart, with all your soul, and with all your mind.' This is the first and great commandment.*

**2. Love Others - 1 Thessalonians 3:12** *And may the Lord make you increase and abound in love to one another and to all, just as we do to you,*

**3. Men, Love Your Wives - Ephesians 5:25-28** *Husbands, love your wives, just as Christ also loved the church and gave Himself for her, that He might sanctify and cleanse her with the washing of water by the word, that He might present her to Himself a glorious church, not having spot or wrinkle or any such thing, but that she should be holy and without blemish. So husbands ought to love their own wives as their own bodies; he who loves his wife loves himself.*

- Do not be harsh with your wife - **Colossians 3:19 (NLT)** *Husbands, love your wives and never treat them harshly.*
- Honor and pray for your wife - **1 Peter 3:7** *Husbands, likewise, dwell with them with*

*understanding, giving honor to the wife, as to the weaker vessel, and as being heirs together of the grace of life, that your prayers may not be hindered.*

## 4. <u>Wives, Love your Husbands and Children</u>

- **Titus 2:4b** . . . *admonish the young women to love their husbands, to*

    *love their children,*

- **1 Peter 3:1-6** *Wives, likewise, be submissive to your own husbands, that even if some do not obey the word, they, without a word, may be won by the conduct of their wives, ² when they observe your chaste conduct accompanied by fear. ³ Do not let your adornment be merely outward--arranging the hair, wearing gold, or putting on fine apparel-- ⁴ rather let it be the hidden person of the heart, with the incorruptible beauty of a gentle and quiet spirit, which is very precious in the sight of God. ⁵ For in this manner, in former times, the holy women who trusted in God also adorned themselves, being submissive to their own husbands, ⁶ as Sarah obeyed Abraham, calling him lord, whose daughters you are if you do good and are not afraid with any terror.*

(The instruction to wives in 1 Peter 3:1 "*that they* [husbands] . . . *may be won*" is applicable not only in attracting a non-believing husband to come to Christ for salvation, but also attracting a believing husband to greater spiritual maturity)

- Win his love (make a daily effort to win his love)
- Win him without a word (without argument or "teaching")
- Win him by your chaste conduct
- Win him by your inner beauty
- Win him with your quiet and gentle spirit

## THREE KINDS OF LOVE FOR CHRISTIAN MARRIAGES

Christians live by **FAITH**—not by FEELINGS. Christian faith involves loving by faith—loving because it is right, because the Lord commands us to love—not loving *only when you feel loving.*

We don't "fall in love." You might fall in a mud puddle or fall for a practical joke, but you do not "fall in love."

People *choose to love,* or they *choose not to love.*

The Christian chooses to love in obedience to Jesus' commands, and by Christ's power at work within him. You can say, "I choose to love you by the power of Christ living in me. I will DO these things written in **1 Corinthians 13:4-8a**; I choose to:

1. Be patient,
2. Be kind.
3. Not envy,
4. Not boast,
5. Not be proud
6. Not be rude,
7. Not insist on my own way,
8. Not be irritable (or irritating),
9. Keep no record of wrongs
10. Not delight in evil
    (and not to delight when evil-doers meet God's justice – Ps. 73:1-22)
11. Rejoice when the Truth wins out
12. Protect my spouse
13. Always respect my spouse,
14. Always expect the best from my spouse,
15. Always persevere.
16. Never give up.

26

The Christian, in love, promises this to his wife or to her husband: I will work together with you to let our "... *conduct be without covetousness; be content with such things as* (we) *have. For* (the Lord) *Himself has said, "I will never leave you nor forsake you."* **Hebrews 13:5**

## THE THREE LOVES

**1. Spiritual love** (Greek word: "*Agape*")

This speaks of your inner spirit; deep, "soul-mate" friendship. Jesus spoke of this kind of love in **Matthew 22:36-40**

*36 "Teacher, which is the great commandment in the law?"*

*37 Jesus said to him, "'You shall love the LORD your God with all your heart, with all your soul, and with all your mind.' 38 This is the first and great commandment. 39 And the second is like it: 'You shall love your neighbor as yourself.' 40 On these two commandments hang all the Law and the Prophets."*

The Apostle Paul wrote of this *agape*-love in **1 Thessalonians 3:12** *And may the Lord make you increase and abound in love to one another and to all, just as we do to you,*

*Agape*-love is the same kind of love toward God described in **Deuteronomy 6:5** *You shall love the LORD*

27

*your God with all your heart, with all your soul, and with all your strength.*

Jesus taught us to practice *agape* love for people in **Matthew 5:43-48**  *"You have heard that it was said, 'You shall love your neighbor and hate your enemy.' ⁴⁴ But I say to you, love your enemies, bless those who curse you, do good to those who hate you, and pray for those who spitefully use you and persecute you, ⁴⁵ that you may be sons of your Father in heaven; for He makes His sun rise on the evil and on the good, and sends rain on the just and on the unjust. ⁴⁶ For if you love those who love you, what reward have you? Do not even the tax collectors do the same? ⁴⁷ And if you greet your brethren only, what do you do more than others? Do not even the tax collectors do so?*
*⁴⁸ Therefore you shall be perfect, just as your Father in heaven is perfect.*

Maintain that deep inner-spirit, "soul-mate" love in your marriage.

## 2. Family Love ("*philadelphia*")

- "*Philadelphia*" is a Bible word that means "brotherly love."
- The kind of love brothers and sisters *should have* for each other
- The kind of love parents *should have* for their children and children for their parents.
- This is a special, growing Family-Love.

Examples:

**Romans 12:10**
*10 Be kindly affectionate to one another with brotherly love, in honor giving preference to one another;*

**1 Thessalonians 4:9**
*9 But concerning brotherly love you have no need that I should write to you, for you yourselves are taught by God to love one another;*

**Hebrews 13:1**
*1 Let brotherly love continue.*

**1 Peter 1:22**
*22 Since you have purified your souls in obeying the truth through the Spirit in sincere love of the brethren, love one another fervently with a pure heart,*

- Every Christian couple should grow in this Family-Love and teach their children to love that way, too, by word and by example.

**3. Romantic Love** (*"eros"*) – Physical love; outward expression of the other two loves

- Although the Greek word, *eros*, is not found in the Bible, we find the concept of this love in both the Old and New Testaments.
- It involves a physical attraction between one man and one woman
- The special physical attraction that is reserved for only the husband/wife relationship
- For only one person—as initiated by God himself in **Genesis 2:24**

  *Therefore a man shall leave his father and mother and be joined to his wife, and they shall become one flesh.*
- Saved only for your spouse – **Job 31:1** "*I have made a covenant with my eyes; Why then should I look upon a young woman?*"
- Sometimes people are so involved here, they sacrifice their Family-Love (*philadelphia*), their spiritual love (*agape*), and their mutual, married friendship.
- Other passages from the Bible that picture this eros-love:

  **Proverbs 5:18-19**
  *18 Let your fountain be blessed, And rejoice with the wife of your youth.*
  *19 As a loving deer and a graceful doe, Let her breasts satisfy you at all times; And always be enraptured with her love.*

**Hebrews 13:4**

[4] Marriage is honorable among all, and the bed undefiled; but fornicators and adulterers God will judge.

**1 Corinthians 6:15-20**

[15] Do you not know that your bodies are members of Christ? Shall I then take the members of Christ and make them members of a harlot? Certainly not! [16] Or do you not know that he who is joined to a harlot is one body with her? For "the two," He says, "shall become one flesh." [17] But he who is joined to the Lord is one spirit with Him.

[18] Flee sexual immorality. Every sin that a man does is outside the body, but he who commits sexual immorality sins against his own body. [19] Or do you not know that your body is the temple of the Holy Spirit who is in you, whom you have from God, and you are not your own? [20] For you were bought at a price; therefore glorify God in your body and in your spirit, which are God's.

**1 Corinthians 7:5**

[5] Do not deprive one another except with consent for a time, that you may give yourselves to fasting and prayer; and come together again so that Satan does not tempt you because of your lack of self-control.

The entire Old Testament book, The Song of Solomon, also is a picture of *eros*-love.

Husbands and wives should have all three loves for each other. Your children should see your love. It should be displayed in the warm way you act toward each other— tender words and behavior, affectionate hugs and kisses, special gifts.

**FOUR Ingredients that should be part of a married couple's Romantic Love (*Eros*)**

**1. Desire to be with each other**

- Husbands and wives should eagerly anticipate having time together.
- David B. Webster in his little book, To Love and To Cherish, wrote: "Time spent together is never wasted."
- This desire to spend time together can be lost.
- If you discover you are missing this ingredient, find ways to put it back.

**2. Concern for each other's well being**

- Husbands and wives should feel each other's joys and discomforts.
- They should take care to protect and comfort each other.

**3. Strong physical attraction for each other**

- Husbands and wives should be attracted to one another visually, by the sound of their voices, and, of course, sexually.

**4. Idealization**

- This means that you see good things in each other that others don't see.

John Shoen, a missionary, was speaking to a small group of servicemen and their wives in Japan. Mr. Shoen passed around a small picture of his wife, and said, "I am married to the most beautiful woman in the world."

The young servicemen and their wives nodded politely as they glanced at the picture of the middle-aged woman, then passed it along.

Mr. Shoen repeated, " I am married to the most beautiful woman in the world." Again there was polite silence.

Finally, he quietly said, "I am married to the most beautiful woman in the world—because she is my wife."

- Idealization is needed for a good marriage to start, but it continues to be needed in a marriage throughout the years.

If any of these ingredients of Romantic love begins to dwindle away in your Christian marriage—you need to work on "re-installing" the missing ingredient.

A couple needs all four of these ingredients.

## PLACE THE LORD AT THE CENTER OF YOUR LOVE

Ask your couple if each of them has a Bible. Learn from them if they have a systematic way of daily Bible reading. If not, offer them a simple method of **reading a portion of God's Word each day**.

**Here is a simple method** for people who may not be avid readers that I picked up years ago and have offered people who do not have any Bible reading pattern:

Read the Gospel of Mark. It is the shortest of the four Gospels, Matthew, Mark, Luke, and John.

Day One: read the first four verses of Mark, chapter one. (Mark 1:1-4)

Day two: again, read the first four verses of Mark 1, and read the next four verses. (Mark 1:1-8)

Each succeeding day, read the last four verses you read the day before, and then next four verses.

It will look like this:

Monday – Mark 1:1-4

Tuesday – Mark 1:1-8

Wednesday – Mark 1:5-12

Thursday – Mark 1:9-16

Friday – Mark 1:13-20

Saturday – Mark 1:17-24, and so on.

It will not take you much time each day. It will not take you many days to read through the Gospel of Mark, and when you complete the Gospel of Mark, you will have read it twice.

Then you can go to another part of the Bible (First John, for instance), and use the same method. Why, you could read the entire Bible that way!

**Encourage your couple to pray together**. I have found that consistently praying together is one of the most difficult things for most couples to do. Maybe it is because of busy schedules, or a natural (but not Godly) spiritual shyness. I don't know.

But if you need to help your couple with this, again offer them a simple way. Perhaps something like this:

At breakfast each day (or, if they don't eat breakfast, suggest they set aside a few minutes before they go their separate ways), take two minutes to do one of four things:

- **Praise/Adoration** – a sentence praising the Lord for something that causes you wonder—His love for you, His Creation, Marriage, Music, etc.

- **Confession of sin** – each of you confess to the Lord some way that you know you are not pleasing Him.

- **Ask** – Often we think of things that we desire that He alone can provide: wisdom, health, children, spiritual maturity, etc.

- **Thanksgiving** – Thank the Lord for the family He has made of you, the health to go to work, your salvation, the income He has given you to work with, etc.

Each subsequent day, choose another of these four things. Rotate through them regularly.

Praying together for two minutes a day is better than not praying together at all.

Remind your couple how important it is to the Lord that they attend a Bible-teaching Church regularly.

35

**Hebrews 10:25 (TLB)**

[25] *Let us not neglect our church meetings, as some people do, but encourage and warn each other, especially now that the day of his coming back again is drawing near.*

To that instruction add an encouragement that your couple build Christian friendships and involve themselves in their local church by using their talents and giftedness to help in church ministry.

## SESSION 3: LET'S COMMUNICATE

A good way to observe the couple's understanding of Christ-like interpersonal communication necessary in marriage is to ask these questions, give them time to think and answer them.

From their answers an observant pastor will learn where he might need to spend some time helping them know how to communicate better.

**What kinds of communication problems do husbands and wives have?**

**What are the results of these communication problems?**

**When do the two of you communicate best together?**

**What helps?**

**What hinders good communication?**

In marriage, communicating well can be a great joy and adventure. Communicating poorly (or not at all) can bring great disappointment into our marriages.

**What improves in our marriages if we are communicating together well?**

Some possible answers:

- o  Problem-solving;
- o  child-rearing;
- o  romance;
- o  dealing with sorrow or trouble;

o spiritual-growth;

o health;

o joy and adventure in life; etc.

**What are some causes of poor communications in marriage?**

Possible answers:

1. Busy-ness
2. Being tired
3. Family tendency to develop different interests
4. Interference of relatives
5. Basic differences of opinions, of backgrounds, etc.
6. Not listening
7. Not talking

**What are some results of poor communication in marriage?**

Possible answers:

1. Misunderstandings
2. Unhappiness
3. Mistrust
4. New companionships (who provide better communication)
5. Drifting into alcoholism, drugs

In order to defend against communication problems becoming major conflicts within your marriage, it is important to remember that **your marriage is more important than either of you getting your own way or winning a point in a discussion.**

**In the event communication conflicts begin to develop, . . .**

## HERE ARE SOME COMMUNICATION-CONFLICT "CURATIVES"

- **Love the Lord. Trust fully in Him.**
    a. Anticipate that *there will be times of conflict* between any two people
    b. Meditate on Matthew 6:25-34, Jesus' instructions
    c. Prepare your attitudes and responses ahead of time for conflicts when they arise. "How am I going to act? Or react? How can I control my emotions rather than having my emotions control me, my words, and my face?"
        - Practice attitudes and actions and responses of kindness at home and at work and at church.
    d. Determine together, and individually, that you will NOT give up on one another—even when you may feel hurt.

(Remember that **your marriage is more important than either of you getting your own way or winning a point in a discussion.**)

    e. Force yourself to *enter back into loving communication,* sacrificially . . . even when you think your spouse should be the one to "go first."

\- **Love each other. Trust each other.**

    a. Go back again and *review 1 Corinthians 13:4-8.*

    b. *Practice* that passage every day of your marriage.

    c. *Work hard* at your love—every day.

**SOME SEED CAUSES OF CONFLICT:**

It is very easy to begin to believe that you have certain "rights" you expect from your marriage partner. It is easy to insist on total control over some possession or place or time. It is easy to expect to develop a mental picture of how you should be treated by your marriage partner.

\- **Remember that your marriage is more important than either of you getting your own way or winning a point in a discussion.**

\- It is better to give away any rights that you feel you are due; or any possessions or expectations that might be causing conflict—give them away to the Lord.

40

**SOLUTION**: Luke 9:23-25

*Then He said to them all, "If anyone desires to come after Me, let him . . .*

1. **deny himself**, *and*
2. **take up his cross**
3. **daily**,
4. *and* **follow Me**. $^{24}$*For whoever desires to save his life will lose it, but whoever loses his life for My sake will save it.* $^{25}$*For what profit is it to a man if he gains the whole world, and is himself destroyed or lost?"*

- **Give all those "rights," "possessions," & "expectations" to the Lord**
- If you receive them back through your spouse— wonderful!
- If your spouse forgets (or is not sensitive enough) to treat you as you have the "right" to be treated, remind the Lord, "That's OK. I gave you my 'rights' anyway. I still love him (her)."
- You could pray, "Lord, You deserved to be treated better than You were, but You gave up those expectations because of Your love for us. If I am *never* treated as I hoped or expected to be treated, by my husband (my wife), I will love him (her) anyway.

   "I give You all my hopes, possessions, and expectations because of my love of my husband (my wife)."

41

- **Surrender your marriage to the Lord.** Your marriage belongs to Him anyway. Your marriage is designed to honor Him. Commit yourself to the Lord's design and honor Him in all you do in marriage.
- **In your marriage, with all of your energy, every day, give to your spouse every kindness and benefit that you can imagine.**

   a. Make your spouse the most important person in your earthly life.

   b. Go to the Lord each day and pray for your spouse.

   c. When working to resolve conflict, if your first attempt doesn't solve the problem, keep trying.

   d. If you quit trying, start trying again.

   e. Always start one more time than you quit.

**Remember that your marriage is more important than either of you getting your own way or winning a point in a discussion.**

## SESSION 4: FINANCES

**Let's start this session on finances by talking about giving to the Lord.**

### WHAT ABOUT TITHING?

Tithing is commanded in the Old Testament. Tithing means to give ten-percent of your income to the Lord.

**Malachi 3:10 (TLB)**

*"Bring all the tithes into the storehouse so there will be enough food in my Temple. If you do," says the Lord Almighty, "I will open the windows of heaven for you. I will pour out a blessing so great you won't have enough room to take it in! Try it! Let me prove it to you!"*

A pastor friend, Phil Cleigh, said, "This is the only commandment in the Bible that I know of, where God makes a promise and challenges us to *prove Him* by obeying it."

My friend might be right. I haven't found another commandment like that.

I have heard people say that the New Testament does not teach tithing. But **Jesus taught tithing** in Matthew 23:23. He was scolding some of the religious leaders of His day for getting their priorities wrong. He said to them,

**Matthew 23:23 (NLT)**

*"How terrible it will be for you teachers of religious law and you Pharisees. Hypocrites! For you are careful to tithe even the tiniest part of your income, but you ignore the important things of the law—justice, mercy, and faith.* **_You should tithe, yes,_** _but you should not leave undone the more important things._

- My understanding is that a Christian should immediately give 10% (of all that God gives to him) to his local church. (Malachi 3:10)
- Then he should give an offering from the 90% which remains.
- Christians should trust the Lord that they can live on the balance.
- Having said that, I know that my faith was small when I began to give to the Lord.
- Some of you may face the same problem.
- We will talk about that in a minute, but first let me give you some thoughts on tithing.

## TITHING

**Short Version:** (Here is a plan that works)

1. Give 10% (or more) to the local church.
2. Save 10% (or more) - for "retirement" or appliances, repairs, etc.
3. Learn to live on 70% of your income

**Now let's flesh this plan out:**

1. **Give 10% (or more) to the local church.** - That is biblical teaching.

   It also makes sense to give to your local church where you are being spiritually fed. After all, you pay the restaurant where you eat. You don't eat at McDonalds and then send your payment to another restaurant that you think needs the money more than McDonalds.

2. **Save 10% (or more)** - The Bible speaks of being wise in handling money, storing up for the future, being generous with money, and taking care not to depend upon, or love, money.[1]

   **Invest for retirement.** Be wise. Seek the advice of biblical financial counselors.

   **Save for purchases** (appliances, cars, etc.). It seems to me better to buy only when you have the money. In buying a home, for example, save while you are renting an apartment, until you have enough cash saved, and then consider whether the house that you want is a good purchase and whether you want to exhaust your savings to buy it. Or would it be prudent to take out a mortgage ("rent" the bank's money) while your savings continues earning interest?

---

[1] Proverbs 3:9-10; 6:6-8; 13:16; 16:2; 21:20; Eccl. 11:2; Matthew 6:25-34; 25:14-30; 1 Timothy 6:17, for a few examples.

See also Appendix #4

Another example of buying when you have the money would be to buy your cars with cash and keep them in good repair. I don't know who told me, "The cheapest car is the one you own," but it has been a good plan for our family.

Another source I read said the best deal on buying cars is to buy a 10-year-old car, drive it for five years, then buy another 10-year-old car.

In any case, it is financially prudent to save and buy when you have the money rather than buying on credit.

### 3. Learn to live on 70% of your income

- Plan
- Set and keep Goals
- Practice financial Discipline

Maybe you think, "Pastor, that little plan of yours only adds up to 90%."

The other 10% serves as a cushion, a buffer. From this you can give an offering, you can build an emergency fund, save for buying gifts, etc. There may even be a necessary expense that you forgot to calculate into your budget.

This simple plan is a place to start. It's better to start somewhere than not to start at all.

Build your plan and work your plan. Start where your faith is, then stretch your faith. If you cannot make ends meet at any point, make an appointment with a trusted financial counselor, or a church leader or a pastor for help. But don't give up your determination to obey the Lord in this matter.

Now let's talk about the difficulty that some of us have with building a money plan, and how to include giving, even tithing, in that plan. As I mentioned before, my faith was small when I began to give to the Lord.

Here's my suggestion: Tithe what you have faith to tithe today.

**2 Corinthians 9:7 (NIV)** *Each man should give what he has decided in his heart to give, not reluctantly or under compulsion, for God loves a cheerful giver.*

The Lord loves a *cheerful* giver. What can you give *cheerfully* to the Lord? Can you *cheerfully* give to the Lord 10% of your . . .
- . . . Gross income?
- . . . Gross income after taxes?
- . . . Take-home pay?
- . . . Take-home pay after taxes?
- . . . Take-home pay after taxes & mortgage?

Whatever 10% you decide that you can *cheerfully* give to the Lord, give it. Tithe something! And do it consistently. Then:
- Set a new goal for next month, or next year.
- Continue to grow in your faith and giving.

- When you have reached the goal of tithing your gross income, add a *giving* goal to your tithes, beyond your tithe.
- Watch God provide the increase.

Sometimes people ask, **Where should my giving go?**

I know of no neat breakdown in Scripture that tells us how to divide our giving to support the many worthy ministries that serve the Lord.

I have already suggested that the first 10% should go to the local church—after that, I would suggest . . .

- Something to your church-supported Missions
- Something more to good ministries outside your church
- A goal of tithes and offerings equal to 20%

## CHECKING ACCOUNTS

Keep your financial records balanced.

Which of you can do that better? He or she should keep the books.

Work together. Learn how to improve.

Don't grow impatient with your plan or with each other.

One joint checking account should be accessible to both of you.

## BUDGET

Good Bible teachers agree that we should have financial standards and a plan for using God's monetary gifts which He entrusts to us. Here are some of my suggestions:

Problems develop with spending, not with earning:

- Determine together to live within your incomes.
- Both of you should have a small pocket allowance.
- Your weekly "Grocery Allowance" should be a regular amount.
- The "Grocery Shopper" should have full freedom to spend the Grocery Allowance.
- Remember: You are teammates, not competitors.
- Resist salesmen and sales pressure.
- General Rule: You cannot afford to buy things from people who come to your home trying to sell you their product.
- The internet has become a competitive marketplace. If you do internet shopping you need to be careful that you are not seduced by sales pressure.
- Be sure that your involvement in the marketplace (stores, Mall, Internet) is considered prayerfully:
  - Decide what you are going to buy, save for it, then go and find the best buy. (Cheapest is not always best.)

**THREATS TO BUDGET** – Can you name some threats to a budget?

Let your couple think and make suggestions, then you might add your own thoughts, such as:

- **Homes or apartments** that are too expensive. One guideline suggests that we spend no more than half of our net income on housing, including utilities.

- The latest **electronic equipment**, gadgets, or "time-saving devices."

- New **cars** (and many used cars) are beyond the range for newly married couples.

- **Credit cards** – If you use them, pay them off each month. Have the money before you "charge it." Don't buy much on credit.

Think of your marriage as a lifelong adventure together to meet your financial needs and stay within your budget.

Keep your credit rating good.

Pay all your bills ahead of time.

## GAMBLING

Gambling is NOT "gaming." A game gives you an equal chance with your opponent to win by your skill.

I have included (Appendix #6) a Scripture study on gambling. With my pre-marriage couples, I simply warn against any gambling and give them a printed copy of <u>The Scripture Study concerning Gambling,</u> Appendix #6.

## SESSION 5: HEALTH, SEXUALITY, INTERPERSONAL RELATIONSHIPS

### HEALTH

Personal Health is a responsibility of the husband for his wife, and of the wife for her husband. Although the following verse is usually applied to sexual intimacy, there is also application to other areas of physically caring for each other:

**1 Corinthians 7:4** *The wife does not have authority over her own body, but the husband does. And likewise the husband does not have authority over his own body, but the wife does.*

**Agree together to eat nutritiously**.

There are many opinions of how healthy and how nutritious Healthy-Nutritious eating is. Learn together. Agree together. Change your opinions when you can do it in agreement.

Here's a simple plan:

Eat fruits, vegetables, grains, and small meat portions.

Drink a lot of water.

Be careful with snack foods and desserts.

**Allow enough time in your schedule for sleep**

This is hard for most young couples. But determine together you are going to invest in some exercise each day.

Then do it. Walk, go to the Y or a gym, whatever works best
for both of you.

- Go to your Doctor for annual physicals and
  discuss any medical problems together and with
  your medical care provider.
- This is especially important before you have
  children.

**SEXUAL INTIMACY**

I want to talk with you frankly about ways of
keeping your intimate life fresh throughout your marriage.
An unscriptural sexual relationship can be an area of
problems in marriage.

> **1 Corinthians 7:2-5 (NIV)** *2 But since there is so
> much immorality, each man should have his own
> wife, and each woman her own husband. 3 The
> husband should fulfill his marital duty to his wife,
> and likewise the wife to her husband. 4 The wife's
> body does not belong to her alone but also to her
> husband. In the same way, the husband's body does
> not belong to him alone but also to his wife. 5 Do not
> deprive each other except by mutual consent and for
> a time, so that you may devote yourselves to prayer.
> Then come together again so that Satan will not tempt
> you because of your lack of self-control.*

Husbands and wives are stewards of each other's
bodies—to protect, care for, love, treat with respect. Sexual

intimacy is an important God-given discipline and joy for married couples.

Here are some important principles for intimacy in a Christian marriage:

### 1. Personal purity

Don't toy with sexual discipline. Determine to avoid flirting with anyone other than your spouse.

Avoid immoral or sexually-suggestive entertainment, perversions, pornographic materials or imaginations. Keep your imagination pure—only for marriage—only for each other.

If there are problems in your sexual discipline, solve them.

### 2. Sexual intimacy is an important part of godly marriage.

Before marriage:

*Where* is the temptation greatest?

Empty house?

Parked car?

Plan to avoid those places until the wedding.

*When* is temptation greatest?

Plan activities with other people during those times. Unavoidable circumstances may tempt you. Escape those circumstances as soon as possible. Detour around them in the future. Plan alternatives.

After the couple is married:

Be faithful to each other sexually and emotionally and in your imagination. **Proverbs 5:18 (NIV)** *May your fountain be blessed, and may you* <u>rejoice in the wife of your youth.</u>

Sexual intimacy is God's seal upon a godly marriage—**Gen. 2:24** *Therefore a man shall leave his father and mother and be joined to his wife, and they shall become one flesh.*

Sex is not a subject for jokes or entertainment. Sexual intimacy is a sacred act of marital unity – a tender event; a joyful event; a private event. It is a covenant from God. (Genesis 2:24, Matthew 19:4-5, Ephesians 5:31)

(After children come, be sure to keep a lock on your bedroom door.)

Normally, sex is a very simple thing. A man is easily aroused—visually, with words, perfume, or memories. So build good memories together.

A woman may or may not be so easily aroused. Before sexual relations begin, a woman normally needs to feel emotionally secure in her marriage, to sense she can trust her husband, and be treated by her husband in genuinely loving ways.

Remember the behaviors of love in 1 Corinthians 13:4-8. It's a husband's privilege and joy to provide emotional security and genuine love to his wife.

In a godly marriage, sexual satisfaction of your mate should be the concern for both of you. Because the husband is easier to satisfy, he has to take extra care to learn what pleases his wife. It is okay throughout your years of marriage to discuss with each other what is pleasurable and what is not. If you don't know, ask.

It is helpful to study a book together that talks about the godly physical relationship within marriage. For example: "INTENDED FOR PLEASURE" by Dr. Ed Wheat and Gaye Wheat

Be careful what you watch (TV, movies, computer) and listen to, and be careful what you meditate on. Stay away from pornography, pornographic thinking, fanaticizing about intimacy with others outside your marriage, or flirting with anyone except your spouse.

Sex should never be used as a weapon or bargaining chip.

If any sinful habits have been part of your pre-married life, confess them to the Lord, ask Him to take away those memories and thoughts, and work at replacing those thoughts with "Philippians 4:8 kinds of thoughts."

**Philippians 4:8**

8 *Finally, brethren, whatever things are true, whatever things are noble, whatever things are just, whatever things are pure, whatever things are lovely, whatever things are of good report, if there is any virtue and if there is anything praiseworthy--meditate on these things.*

Over the years of your marriage be aware that emotional and physical changes may take place that may affect intimacy.

If a time comes when through illness or injury or for other reasons sexual relations are not possible, your marriage should be strong enough emotionally and spiritually to continue to strengthen in spite of the loss. Remain faithful to the Lord and to each other.

### 3. Birth control (after marriage)

There are **many kinds of birth control** available, if you choose to use them.

Condoms are convenient and easy to use. When purchasing condoms, look for lubricated styles.

It is also good to have a water-soluble lubricant in your bedroom, such as "K-Y Jelly" (or liquid)

**Birth control pills**: Discuss side effects with a doctor before you use them.

What about **permanent birth control**?

Agree together if you are considering a permanent pregnancy-preventative measure (e.g., vasectomy or tubal ligation). Make your choice a matter of prayer and make your choice subject to the leading of the Lord.

Honor one another in the choice you have agreed upon together. Agree not to blame each other if you choose to make a permanent change, then regret that decision later.

It is very easy for most women to become pregnant. Birth control should be planned ahead, kept convenient.

- **God does not allow for abortion (Psalm 139:13-16).**
- An unplanned child will be loved as much as a planned one.

**4. For older couples—or second marriages:**

    a. Deal honestly and openly about your first marriage(s).

    b. Put away fantasies about previous relationships or marriages.

    c. Be faithful to each other.

    d. Develop your "best friendship" with each other.

## INTERPERSONAL AND SOCIAL RELATIONSHIPS

Make allowance in your communication together for the fact that we are all subject to cycles of emotion—some of us more than others.

Be sensitive and gentle with each other.

Work to maintain positive attitudes in your marriage.

Communicate openly on many subjects. Learn to listen. Develop each other's strengths. Don't try to change each other. (You will discover areas you would *like* to change.)

Admire each other. Accept your spouse as he or she is. Allow your spouse to be different than you are, to hold different opinions, to be the individual God has made him to be. And admire those differences between you. Build each other.

Don't solve problems after 10 pm. If there is a "dead-locked disagreement" and you are both weary of trying to find a resolution, make an appointment to take up the discussion the next day, then get a good night's rest.

Work hard together to build friendships with other people and to make those social friendships good.

Don't make fun of your spouse in public or to your friends.

When you are with family members or friends, don't tell stories about your spouse in a funny way. (Unless you have explicit permission from your spouse to tell the story)

## GETTING ALONG WITH YOUR EXTENDED FAMILY

When two people marry, two families come together. When you leave your parents and become one with your husband/wife, your families will feel the loss to a greater or a lesser degree. You need your family independence, but be gracious. Make your marriage a gain for your families.

Work hard TOGETHER to get along with both of your families. It is more important that you learn to understand your parents and in-laws than it is that they understand you.

Plan visits to both families regularly, at least at holiday times. Plan always to go TOGETHER to visit family.

If there are social, ethnic, or religious differences between your families, or between you and your families, work hard to understand, and to be hospitable.

You can be sacrificial with your time and energy to get along with your extended families. Remember, the Lord gave His life for you.

## CHURCH LIFE

Don't forget the Lord in your marriage.

*Make a habit of regular church attendance.* You should not have to decide *if* you are going to go to church. Make it your habit that on Sunday, you will be at church. On time. Your children will adopt your habit.

Develop a schedule that will get you to church early. Christian author Henrietta Mears said, "If you're not ten minutes early, you're late."

Pastor's wife and author Anne Ortland wrote, "The idea is to express eagerness. If you stand around yakking outside, you give off the aroma that you consider meeting people more important than meeting God."

Get to know your church family well. Become involved in ministering together with your church family.

**PERSONAL DEVOTIONAL LIFE**

Read the Scripture and pray together at least once a week. Make this a permanent part of your marriage. Restart as often as is necessary. It may be helpful to have a Bible at your dining room table. Before you eat breakfast (or any meal) read a short portion of scripture and pray.

**ROMANCE**

Make romance a regular part of your schedule. Keep dating each other. Don't allow money to be an issue. There are ways to have dates that cost little or nothing. Just ask some of your older friends what they did for dates when they were first married and poor.

Keep times guarded to use for dates.

Select reading, music, television and other entertainment for your home which honor God, honor marriage, honor the creative mind God gave you, and honor the romance that keeps your marriage fresh.

## POST-MARITAL COUNSELING

Invite your pastor and his wife into your home about a month after your wedding to share with them the joys and surprises of married life. Do it again after about six months of marriage.

Remember, you can call your pastor any time. It is always better to visit with your pastor before any problem grows serious.

## SESSION 6: CONTROLLING ANGER

What does the Bible say about anger?

In **Ephesians 4:26** the Bible says three things about being angry.

1. **BE ANGRY**

   - ASK: What is anger?

     ANSWER: Anger is an "emotion." The word "emotion" is two words glued together: "**e**" meaning 'to,' plus "**motion**" meaning 'move.' An emotion is designed *to move* us.

   - Anger itself is not a sin. It is a God-given, powerful motivator.

   - VINCENT'S Word Studies of the New Testament say: "*Righteous anger is commanded; not merely permitted.*"

   - Anger has its place as a motivator for good.

   - BUT because anger is so powerful, it is also dangerous.

   - AND anger *should not* become a habit—

     But only an <u>occasional incident</u>—

     Kept under control—

       driving you to do good.

The second thing **Ephesians 4:26** says about anger:

2. **DO NOT SIN**

   - When we are angry, we have a choice:

     to act sinfully, or

     to act without sinning.

64

- Our natural (human) inclination when we are angry is to react sinfully.
- Remember the Lord.
- Imitate the Lord.
- ASK: When does anger turn to sin?
- POSSIBLE ANSWERS:

    When we brood against someone who has wronged us.

    When we create and hold grudges.

    When we continue to rehearse the hurt someone has caused us.

- When our anger *does* turn to sin, as with any other sin, we must confess our sin and turn away from it (repent).
- **1 John 1:9** *If we confess our sins, He is faithful and just to forgive us our sins and to cleanse us from all unrighteousness.*

    **Acts 3:19** *Repent therefore and be converted, that your sins may be blotted out, so that times of refreshing may come from the presence of the Lord,*

The third thing **Ephesians 4:26** says about anger:

### 3. DO NOT LET THE SUN GO DOWN ON YOUR WRATH.

- This phrase is telling us how seriously God expects us to handle anger in our lives.

65

- Deal with anger concretely, definitely, resolutely, decisively, absolutely and "in no uncertain terms."
- Deal with anger quickly, immediately.

Anger is a God-given motivator you want to use quickly and correctly, to do good, to be constructive, then dispose of it.

Anger is like a lit stick of dynamite in your hand. You need to decide quickly what to do with your anger and do what is right. Do it quickly, before it explodes and becomes destructive.

There is only one place I *know* where the Bible specifically says that Jesus was angry. We find that in **Mark 3:1-5**.

In other passages we read that Jesus overturned the tables of the money-changers in the temple. (John 2:13-17) He *may* have been angry then, but the Bible doesn't specifically say so. At the time of that incident, Jesus' disciples remembered an Old Testament quotation, Psalm 69:9, *Because zeal for Your house has eaten me up, . . .*

*Zeal* is another word for emotion. Jesus had apparently shown strong emotion in the temple. That emotion might have been anger. Or, it might have been sorrow, disappointment, or some other strong emotion. We are not told.

But in **Mark 3:1-5** we know for sure Jesus was angry, because the Bible tells us so. Have your couple follow in their Bibles as you read the passage in Mark 3:1-5.

ASK: "What three things did Jesus DO with His anger?" (Mark 3:5)

Give them time to discover those three things. Help them when you need to.

ANSWERS:     In His anger, Jesus:

    v. 5 – "looked around at his enemies" (Was that sinful?)

- "grieved" for His enemies (Was that sinful?)
- healed the man with the crippled hand  (Was that sinful?)

Jesus was angry. But He did not sin in His anger. He did not let the sun go down on His anger. He used His anger to do good; and He did it quickly.

ASK: What can we do when we are angry that is NOT sin?

For instance, what can you do when you hit your thumb with a hammer?

Some possible answers, when your couple needs suggestions:

> Change your hammering technique
> Practice to improve hand-eye coordination
> Go to the hospital for treatment
> "Are those things sinful?"

67

What can you do when a fellow-employee criticizes your work?

Possible answers:

Examine your work:

"Is my critic right? partly-right? or wrong?"

"Is there something in my life I need to change?"

From time to time a pastor may get comments or notes about how to be a better pastor. If he considers the comment, the pastor can usually discover something that helps him, once he gets over his self-pity.

Examine your relationship with that fellow-employee:

Have you been Christ-like toward him?

Can you be a better friend to him?

Is there something he needs? Is he crying out for your help?

What can you do when a family member does not treat you right? (Husband, wife, child, parent, etc.)

Possible answers:

Forgive him or her

Examine *your role* in the family as a husband (or wife, or father, or mother, or child)

What does God's Word say about the way a (husband, wife, parent, child) should live?

When you become angry, try to quickly remember that anger is a God-given motivator to do good. But, as a motivator, anger must be handled quickly and correctly.

**There is something else the Bible says about Anger** that emphasizes the importance of taking care of that emotion quickly and correctly.

**Ephesians 4:31** *Let all bitterness, wrath, anger, clamor, and evil speaking be put away from you, with all malice.*

Here God shows us . . .

**A Progressive Development of anger which needs to be broken** as early as possible:

> **BITTERNESS** - internal, acidy frame of mind
>
> **WRATH** - quick temper, short fuse
>
> **ANGER** - enduring, violent outward expression
>
> **CLAMOR** - loud quarreling
>
> **EVIL - SPEAKING** - abusive, hate-filled speech, cursing and worse (blasphemy)
>
> **MALICE** - vicious, evil intentions

You will notice the destructive progression in this list, from milder to more severe forms of anger. You may discover yourself in this progressive list. The key is to break this chain as early as possible.

In prison visits I have made, I have often noticed that inmates are incarcerated because they have allowed this progression to develop until, in violent anger, they did what they should not have done.

Social groups, media, military training, gangs, political gatherings, even athletic teams or coaches will sometimes *encourage* progressive anger or rage to motivate their members.

It might work in combative competition, but it is not biblical. It does not work well in marriage and family relationships.

When you become angry, try to quickly remember that anger is a God-given motivator to do good. Take control of your anger. Don't let it take control of you.

Use it to do good. Do so quickly and correctly.

Then be rid of the anger.

Don't brood over wrongs done to you.

Don't hold a grudge.

Don't even remember it. God doesn't remember your confessed and forsaken sins against Him. He says, *"Their sins and their lawless deeds I will remember no more."*

**Hebrews 10:17**

God chooses not to remember the sins of those who have confessed their sins to Him and forsaken them. God is the Example we need to follow when someone wrongs us. In your anger do good, and do it quickly.

Then determine not to remember the sins others have committed against you.

Don't meditate on them.

Don't re-enact or rehearse the hurt.

Don't recite it to others.

Forgive. Put it out of your memory. Choose not to rehearse it, repeat it, or think about it.

Sometimes that takes God's help. Ask Him for it, and then do it.

## SESSION 7: DEALING WITH CONFLICT IN MARRIAGE

Conflicts are inevitable in human relationships. Marriage is no exception. Thank the Lord for His Word with which He directs us what to do in times of conflict.

Thank Him for His Holy Spirit Who enables us, as followers of Jesus, to do right when conflict arises.

In Scripture-teaching about how to resolve conflict an important principle to remember is this:

### THE AIM IS ALWAYS RECONCILIATION

The purpose of biblical counseling is to lay a strong foundation for your marriage. A marriage foundation to last a lifetime.

Recognize that anything that you do in Christ's name as you deal with conflict between yourself and anyone else (including family members) needs to be a **ministry of reconciliation**.

In a Christian marriage if the conflict becomes so dangerous that there is need for a physical separation—that separation is for safety and for time to figure out **a way to reconcile**. Separation is not intended to be a time to try a new freedom from marriage.

**The aim is always reconciliation.**

Divorce is never commanded in the Scripture and is permitted only for unfaithfulness or habitual immorality. Divorce is a sorrowful end to a long series of failed efforts to reconcile.

In **Matthew 18:15-20**, the Lord gives us His plan for reconciling interpersonal conflicts. His plan should be applied to conflicts within a marriage.

## A MINISTRY OF RECONCILIATION IN MARRIAGE
### 2 Corinthians 5:20

*We are therefore Christ's ambassadors, as though God were making his appeal through us. We implore you on Christ's behalf: **Be reconciled** to God.*

If a husband and a wife are reconciled to God, they will find ways of reconciling with each other.

## JESUS' INSTRUCTIONS FOR RECONCILING A CONFLICT between a married Christian couple are clearly and simply given in **Matthew 18:15-20**,

*"If your brother sins against you, go and show him his fault, just between the two of you. If he listens to you, you have won your brother over. [16]But if he will not listen, take one or two others along, so that 'every matter may be established by the testimony of two or three witnesses.' [17]If he refuses to listen to them, tell it to the church; and if he refuses to listen even to the church, treat him as you would a pagan or a tax collector.*

*[18]"I tell you the truth, whatever you bind on earth will be bound in heaven, and whatever you loose on earth will be loosed in heaven.*

*[19]"Again, I tell you that if two of you on earth agree about anything you ask for, it will be done for you by my Father in heaven. [20]For where two or three come together in my name, there am I with them."*

1. **The first step of reconciliation is for the offended party to go to the offender, privately, and try to agree together. (Mt. 18:15)**

   If this first step is handled biblically, many conflicts are resolved. If not, the conflicts can grow worse.

   **Matthew 18:15** *Moreover if your brother sins against you, go and tell him his fault between you and him alone. If he hears you, you have gained your brother.*

   a. *"between you and him alone"* – Keep the "circle" small. In marriage conflict, keep it between husband and wife. There is a great temptation to share the problem with close friends or family members. Try to NOT do that.

   If it has already been shared, your problem may have an added complication. When your marriage conflict is reconciled, you will have the added problem of resolving your marriage conflict in the minds of those you let into your inner circle.

b. A large percentage of conflicts between Christian husbands and wives will be resolved in this first step as the couple works through their disagreements and conflicts together, with their aim being reconciliation.

c. Don't brood. Don't build a grudge. Don't entertain thoughts of revenge. *"Go and tell him his fault between you and him alone."*

d. Carefully craft the language and the attitudes you will use when you go to talk with your spouse. Use language that does not make the conflict worse, but encourages reconciliation, remembering that the aim is always reconciliation.

If the conflict continues unresolved, proceed to the second step:

**2. The second step is for the offended party to take one or two others with him to the offender and together try to reconcile.**

a. This is an instruction to seek help from one or two godly counselors. **Matthew 18:16** *But if he will not hear, take with you one or two more, that 'by the mouth of two or three witnesses every word may be established.'*

b. The selection of the *"one of two others"* should be people that both you and your spouse respect, trust, and admire.

c. I have often thought that Jesus, in His fore-wisdom was implying that the "*one or two others*," might be older, godly, married friends who have a good, biblical marriage; perhaps your pastor and his wife; or marriage counselors that have a strong, Christ-centered marriage.

d. In any case, these "*one or two others*" need to be strong believers in Bible teaching for marriage.

e. Notice the "circle" of involvement is still being kept small.

f. Never forget, <u>the aim is always reconciliation.</u>

3. **The third step is to take the matter to the church**

   **Matthew 18:17a** *And if he refuses to hear them, tell it to the church.*

   a. I believe *this does not mean* to gossip it through the church body or to make an announcement in a church service or in a venue for prayer requests.

   b. I believe that Jesus refers here to the leadership of the church, to the pastor and the elders (deacons), appealing to them for help to reconcile the disagreement or offence.

c.  This instruction is for husband and wife both to submit to church leadership for help, for biblical instruction.

d.  The church leaders might counsel the husband and wife concerning their financial situation. Finances are a leading cause of marriage conflict. Or, they may do some anger-management counseling. Or, send the couple to a marriage retreat (Fairhaven Ministries in Tennessee, for example). Or something else.

e.  Keep remembering, <u>the aim is always reconciliation</u>.

**4. Finally, if the problem is not resolved by these first 3 steps, Jesus says in Matthew 15:17b . . .** *But if he refuses even to hear the church, let him be to you like a heathen and a tax collector.*

a.  Does that sound harsh and "un-Jesus-like?"

b.  It might *seem* harsh until you think about Jesus Himself.

c.  ASK: How did Jesus treat heathen and tax collectors?

i.  Let the couple think and answer.

ii.  Then confirm that Jesus *loved* "heathen and tax collectors." He consistently tried to woo them into

His Kingdom. His love for them took
Jesus to the Cross.

d.  The Aim is Always Reconciliation.

e.  This instruction means that the resolution of
this conflict, having reached this point, might
require *a long, faithful journey* loving an
offending spouse and doing all possible, even
sacrificially, to win him (her) back.

f.  I have known marriages where one spouse
becomes a Christian, but the other spouse
resists spiritual commitment to Jesus. I have
seen that Christian spouse faithfully love
and, in a Christ-like manner, do everything
possible to win the marriage-mate to the
Lord. For years.

g.  This step means that in an un-reconciled
conflict, the Christian spouse (and they may
both be Christians, even if they are in
conflict) needs to treat the other as Jesus
would treat a non-believer, lovingly and
patiently trying to win them back.

h.  Notice this example from Jesus' life:

**Matthew 9:10-13** *While Jesus was having dinner at
Matthew's house, many tax collectors and sinners came and
ate with him and his disciples. [11] When the Pharisees saw
this, they asked his disciples, "Why does your teacher eat
with tax collectors and 'sinners'?"*

*[12]On hearing this, Jesus said, "It is not the healthy who need a doctor, but the sick. [13]But go and learn what this means: 'I desire mercy, not sacrifice.' For I have not come to call the righteous, but sinners."*

**The aim is always reconciliation.**
(See also Mt. 15:22-28, and Luke 19:1-10)
**Luke 19:10** *For the Son of Man came to seek and to save what was lost."*

In this instruction, treating your spouse-in-conflict the way Jesus treated "heathen and tax collectors," you have an opportunity to begin a new, strong and long-term ministry in your marriage—a ministry of reconciliation.

5.  **The last two verses in this passage instruct you never to quit praying <u>for</u>** (not against) **your husband/wife, even in times of conflict. (Mt. 18:18-19)**

    -   In our Christian marriages, we have two objectives to keep in mind as we deal with conflict.
    -   First, we want to stop any sin *in our own lives.*
    -   Second, we want to *reconcile* with our spouse.

## A WARNING TO ALL OF US:

**Galatians 6:1-5** *Brothers, if someone is caught in a sin, you who are spiritual should restore him gently. But watch yourself, or you also may be tempted. [2]Carry each other's burdens, and in this way you will fulfill the law of Christ. [3]If anyone thinks he is something when he is nothing, he deceives himself. [4]Each one should test his own actions. Then he can take pride in himself, without comparing himself to somebody else, [5]for each one should carry his own load.*

**SOME FINAL REMINDERS FOR YOUR PRE-MARRIAGE COUPLE**

**HAVE YOU TAKEN CARE OF . . .?**

1. Marriage license?

2. A good photographer?

3. Reception? Caterer?

4. Rehearsal supper or "Groom's Supper"? Will it be before or after the rehearsal?

5. Musicians?

6. Special music?

7. Do you want a bulletin? Who will prepare it?

8. Is your Order of Service complete, the way you want your wedding to look?

9. Are there any special features in your Order of Service you are going to add or change?

10. Guest list – who are you going to invite? Will you send invitations? In a church wedding are you going to invite the congregation?

**HOW NOT TO BE NERVOUS DURING THE WEDDING:**

1. Decide everything before rehearsal. (Your pastor will enforce that at rehearsal.)

2. Rely on your pastor to remember the entire service. You enjoy it. Your pastor will "do" the service for you, and tell you what to do, and when.

3. If pictures are taken before the ceremony, do it EARLY. No last-minute rushing around as people begin to arrive. (It is better, in most cases, to have pictures taken after the ceremony.)

# BOOK 2

## REFRESHER FOR HUSBANDS, REFRESHER FOR WIVES

Some married couples may have forgotten their pre-marriage counseling, if indeed they received any. The foundational biblical principles used in pre-marriage counseling are essential to build strong and lasting marriages. These same principles may be used to refresh and revitalize strained marriages.

Here we have taken pre-marriage counseling principles and placed them in a form to be used with already married couples.

This may be used in Marriage Counseling, in a Bible Study, or used by married couples to improve their relationship in a biblical way.

### INTRODUCTION TO MARRIAGE, AGAIN

(Pastor, ask these questions and jot some notes as you learn more about your couple.)

NAMES:

AGES:

ADDRESSES:


PHONES:

HOW DID YOU MEET?

WHERE ARE YOU IN YOUR SPIRITUAL JOURNEY?

(Gospel track - What do these verses say to you?)

Rom. 3:23

Rom. 6:23

John 14:6

1 Corinthians 15:3 - Why did Jesus die on the cross?

John 1:12

1 John 1:9

Rom. 10:9


WHY ARE YOU COMING TO A PASTOR RATHER THAN ANOTHER COUNSELOR?


COMMON INTERESTS? HOBBIES?


DESCRIBE YOUR SPOUSE FOR ME:

Interests –

Values –

Strengths –

Areas that need work –

(Pastor, this next section begins to re-establish foundational truths for Christian marriage that are essential. Your couple may not remember that anyone talked with them about these truths before.)

## SESSION 1: SCRIPTURAL BACKGROUND FOR MARRIAGE

**Ephesians 5:31-33** - Why marriage is so important:

These verses show us that God's intention is to paint in each marriage a picture of the relationship between Christ and His Church.

- The Man is to care for and love his wife sacrificially, as Christ cares for and loves His Bride, the Church.
- The Woman is called to lovingly respond to her husband, just as the Church (the body of believers who love and trust the Lord Jesus) responds with faithful love for Christ.

Marriage involves **submission to each other**.

**Ephesians 5:21** . . . *submitting to one another in the fear of God.*

"Submission" - a positive or a negative word?

The beauty of "submission" and "authority" is found in the relationship between God as Father and as Son.

**Philippians 2:5-11** *5 Let this mind be in you which was also in Christ Jesus,* (**the Son**) *6 who, being in the form of God,*

85

*did not consider it robbery to be equal with God,* **(the Father)** *⁷ but made Himself of no reputation,* **(the Son submitted to the Father by)** *taking the form of a bondservant, and coming in the likeness of men. ⁸ And being found in appearance as a man, He humbled Himself and became obedient to the point of death, even the death of the cross.*

*⁹ Therefore God also has highly exalted Him and given Him the name which is above every name, ¹⁰ that at the name of Jesus every knee should bow, of those in heaven, and of those on earth, and of those under the earth,*

*¹¹ and that every tongue should confess that Jesus Christ is Lord, to the glory of God the Father.*

"Submission" means: Marriage is not a 50-50 relationship, but both husband and wife *give* 100% of themselves to one another as long as they both shall live. The character quality of "selflessness" is essential in a Christian marriage.

Submission means identifying your God-given role (as husband or as wife) and fitting into that role biblically. Submission means serving each other, not demanding service from one another.

Submission involves Self-less-ness:

Giving up selfish expectations.

Disposing of non-Biblical attitudes and ideas.

86

Ask yourselves, "Where might non-Biblical attitudes and ideas come from?" Think about that question. Discuss it between yourselves.

Non-Biblical attitudes can come from *TV, internet, well-meaning friends, literature (both factual and fiction), school, and even your own inner thoughts.* But wherever they come from, if brought into the marriage circle, non-Biblical attitudes and ideas will corrode the marriage bond.

It is easy to adopt (without realizing we are doing it) the attitudes and words and phrases and jokes that you hear from *TV drama and comedy, romance literature, radio and TV talk shows, internet sites, popular self-help or marriage analytical books or articles, social networking, even the news media.* Well-meaning friends who are not familiar with their Bibles can give damaging, non-Biblical counsel to us.

**A few practices to intentionally avoid** include:

- talking in negative ways about your spouse to him (her), or to other people;

- making jokes or telling embarrassing stories about your spouse unless you have express permission to "tell that story."

God's design for marriage involves a husband and a wife practicing <u>sacred respect and honor</u> toward each another.

Let's talk about Teamwork in your marriage:

Work at understanding each other.

AVOID:

1) Discussing your marriage or your spouse with friends or family members, or with people at work.

2) phrases such as: "What's that supposed to mean?"

THINK:

1) the best of each other

2) the best of one another's intentions and motives

**WHAT IS LOVE** (according to God' Word)?

As you read the following passage, listen for anything in this passage that seems different from the way that we normally think about love.

**1 Corinthians 13:4-8**

4 *Love suffers long and is kind; love does not envy; love does not parade itself, is not puffed up;*

5 *does not behave rudely, does not seek its own, is not provoked, thinks no evil;*

6 *does not rejoice in iniquity, but rejoices in the truth;*

7 *bears all things, believes all things, hopes all things, endures all things.*

8 *Love never fails. . .*

Read the passage, then think about it. Is there anything about *God's description* of love that seems different from the way we think about love? Give yourself a moment to think. You may or may not notice an answer.

ANSWER: God's idea of love does not deal directly with *emotions* like our ideas of love often do. This passage tells us that *love is active*. All of these phrases are *action phrases*.

**1 Corinthians 13:4-8a (NIV)**

1. Be patient,
2. Be kind.
3. Do not envy,
4. Do not boast,
5. Don't be proud
6. Don't be rude,
7. Don't insist on your own way,
8. Don't be irritable (or irritating),
9. Keep no record of wrongs
10. Do not delight in evil (or when evil-doers meet God's justice – Ps. 73:1-22)
11. Rejoice when the Truth wins out
12. Protect, *to roof over; to cover with silence* – (Strong's Concordance)
13. Always respect a person,
14. Always expect the best from a person,
15. Always persevere.
16. Never quit, nor give up. (v. 8a)

This passage describes the character and behavior of God-given love—what love *is*. It does so by describing what love *does*. Love *acts* this way.

That's why you can keep your marriage vows. Even if you are upset with each other, you can love—you can *behave* as God tells you to in this passage.

89

Married couples would do well to print this list and put it on their refrigerator. Each morning you should ask the Lord to help you love as God tells us to love. At the end of each day you could go down the list, evaluating how you have done. "Did this well. Did this well. Oops, not so good here. I need to work on this one. Etc."

A husband or a wife could do this all their lives and continually grow in Christ-like love.

End this session with these few words of wisdom for building good marriage relations together.

1. Always be trustworthy. Keep your word. Keep appointments.

    Keep your promises.

2. Trust one another.

3. Your love must be tough.

    Difficult times will come.

    When then do, work together.

    Help each other. Comfort one another.

**SESSION 2: FOUNDATIONAL LOVES FOR A LONG
MARRIAGE**

Here are some verses to use in helping you realize
what it means to have a fully rounded love-life as designed
for you by the Lord Himself.

1. **Love the Lord** - **Matthew 22:37-38** *Jesus said to him,
"'You shall love the LORD your God with all your heart, with
all your soul, and with all your mind.' This is the first and
great commandment.*

2. **Love Others** - **1 Thessalonians 3:12** *And may the Lord
make you increase and abound in love to one another and to
all, just as we do to you,*

3. **Men, Love Your Wives** - **Ephesians 5:25-28** *Husbands,
love your wives, just as Christ also loved the church and
gave Himself for her, that He might sanctify and cleanse her
with the washing of water by the word, that He might
present her to Himself a glorious church, not having spot or
wrinkle or any such thing, but that she should be holy and
without blemish. So husbands ought to love their own wives
as their own bodies; he who loves his wife loves himself.*
- Do not be harsh with your wife. **Colossians 3:19
  (NLT)** *Husbands, love your wives and never treat
  them harshly.*
- Honor; pray for your wife. **1 Peter 3:7**
  *Husbands, likewise, dwell with them with*

91

understanding, giving honor to the wife, as to the weaker vessel, and as being heirs together of the grace of life, that your prayers may not be hindered.

## 4. Wives, Love your Husbands and Children - Titus 2:4b

. . . admonish the young women to love their husbands, to love their children,

- **1 Peter 3:1-6** Wives, likewise, be submissive to your own husbands, that even if some do not obey the word, they, without a word, may be won by the conduct of their wives, 2 when they observe your chaste conduct accompanied by fear. 3 Do not let your adornment be merely outward--arranging the hair, wearing gold, or putting on fine apparel-- 4 rather let it be the hidden person of the heart, with the incorruptible beauty of a gentle and quiet spirit, which is very precious in the sight of God. 5 For in this manner, in former times, the holy women who trusted in God also adorned themselves, being submissive to their own husbands, 6 as Sarah obeyed Abraham, calling him lord, whose daughters you are if you do good and are not afraid with any terror.

- Win his love (make a daily effort to win his love)
- Win him without a word
- Win him by your chaste conduct

92

- Win him by your inner beauty
- Win him with your quiet and gentle spirit


Win him to the Lord. (Apply this not only in attracting a non-believing husband to come to Christ for salvation, but also attracting a believing husband to greater spiritual maturity. Or to win a refreshment of his love for you by your Christ-likeness.)

## BIBLICAL LOVE FOR CHRISTIAN MARRIAGES

Christians live by **FAITH**—not by FEELINGS. Christian faith involves loving by faith—loving because it is right, because the Lord commands us to love—not loving *only when you feel loving.*

We don't "fall in love." You might fall in a mud puddle or fall for a practical joke, but you do not "fall in love."

People *choose* to love, or they *choose* not to love.

The Christian chooses to love in obedience to Jesus' commands, and by His power at work within him. You can say, "I choose to love you by the power of Christ living in me. I will DO these things written in 1 Corinthians 13:4-8a.

I choose to:

1. Be patient,
2. Be kind.
3. Not envy,
4. Not boast,
5. Not be proud

6. Not be rude,
7. Not insist on my own way,
8. Not be irritable (or irritating),
9. Keep no record of wrongs
10. Not delight in evil
    (and not to delight when evil-doers meet God's justice – Ps. 73:1-22)
11. Rejoice when the Truth wins out
12. Protect my spouse, ('bears all things' means *to roof over; to cover with silence*)
13. Always respect my spouse,
14. Always expect the best from my spouse,
15. Always persevere.
16. Never give up. (v. 8 '*Love never fails,*' or '*never quits*')

The Christian, in love, promises this to his wife or to her husband: I will work together with you to let our . . . *conduct be without covetousness; be content with such things as* (we) *have. For* (the Lord) *Himself has said, "I will never leave you nor forsake you."* **Hebrews 13:5**

**THREE (3) Kinds of Love** needed in Christian Marriage

**1. Spiritual love** (Greek word: "*Agape*")

This speaks of your inner spirit; deep, "soul-mate" friendship. Jesus spoke of this kind of love in **Matthew 22:36-40**

> *36 "Teacher, which is the great commandment in the law?"*

> *37 Jesus said to him, "'You shall love the LORD your God with all your heart, with all your soul, and with all your mind.' 38 This is the first and great commandment. 39 And the second is like it: 'You shall love your neighbor as yourself.' 40 On these two commandments hang all the Law and the Prophets."*

The Apostle Paul wrote of this *agape*-love in **1 Thessalonians 3:12** *And may the Lord make you increase and abound in love to one another and to all, just as we do to you,*

*Agape*-love is the same kind of love toward God described in **Deuteronomy 6:5** *You shall love the LORD your God with all your heart, with all your soul, and with all your strength.*

Jesus taught us to practice *agape*-love for people in **Matthew 5:43-48** *"You have heard that it was said, 'You shall love your neighbor and hate your enemy.' 44 But I say to you, love your enemies, bless those who curse you, do good to those who hate you, and pray for those who* spitefully use you and persecute you, <sup>45</sup> that you may be sons of your Father in heaven; for He makes His sun rise on the evil and on the good, and sends rain on the just and on the unjust. <sup>46</sup> For if you love those who love you, what reward have you? Do not even the tax collectors do the same? <sup>47</sup> And if you greet your brethren only, what do you do more than others? Do not even the tax collectors do so?

<sup>48</sup> Therefore you shall be perfect, just as your Father in heaven is perfect.

Maintain that deep inner-spirit, "soul-mate" love in your marriage.

**2. Family Love** ("*philadelphia*")
- "*Philadelphia*" is a Bible word that means "brotherly love."
- The kind of love brothers and sisters *should have* for each other
- The kind of love parents *should have* for their children and children for their parents.
- This is a special, growing Family-Love.

Examples:

**Romans 12:10** *Be kindly affectionate to one another with brotherly love, in honor giving preference to one another;*

**1 Thessalonians 4:9** *But concerning brotherly love you have no need that I should write to you, for you yourselves are* *taught by God to love one another;*

**Hebrews 13:1** *Let brotherly love continue.*

**1 Peter 1:22** *Since you have purified your souls in obeying the truth through the Spirit in sincere love of the brethren, love one another fervently with a pure heart,*

- Every Christian couple should grow in this Family-Love and teach their children to love that way, too, by word and by example.

**3. Romantic Love** (*"eros"*) – Physical love; outward expression of the other two loves

- Although the Greek word, *eros*, is not found in the Bible, we find the concept of this love in both the Old and New Testaments.
- It involves a physical attraction between one man and one woman
- The special physical attraction that is reserved for only the husband/wife relationship
- For only one person—as initiated by God himself in **Genesis 2:24**
  *Therefore a man shall leave his father and mother and be joined to his wife, and they shall become one flesh.*

- Saved only for your spouse – **Job 31:1** *"I have made a covenant with my eyes; Why then should I look upon a young woman?"*
- Sometimes people are so involved here, they sacrifice their Family-Love (*philadelphia*), their spiritual love (agape), and their mutual, married friendship.
- Other passages from the Bible that picture this *eros-love*:

**Proverbs 5:18-19** *Let your fountain be blessed, And rejoice with the wife of your youth. ¹⁹ As a loving deer and a graceful doe, Let her breasts satisfy you at all times; And always be enraptured with her love.*

**Hebrews 13:4** *Marriage is honorable among all, and the bed undefiled; but fornicators and adulterers God will judge.*

**1 Corinthians 6:15-20** *Do you not know that your bodies are members of Christ? Shall I then take the members of Christ and make them members of a harlot? Certainly not! ¹⁶ Or do you not know that he who is joined to a harlot is one body with her? For "the two," He says, "shall become one flesh." ¹⁷ But he who is joined to the Lord is one spirit with Him.*

*¹⁸ Flee sexual immorality. Every sin that a man does is outside the body, but he who commits sexual immorality sins against his own body. ¹⁹ Or do you not know that your body is the temple of the Holy Spirit who is in you, whom you have from God, and you are not your own? ²⁰ For you were*

98

*bought at a price; therefore glorify God in your body and in your spirit, which are God's.*

**1 Corinthians 7:5** *Do not deprive one another except with consent for a time, that you may give yourselves to fasting and prayer; and come together again so that Satan does not tempt you because of your lack of self-control.*

The entire Old Testament book, <u>The Song of Solomon</u>, also is a picture of *eros*-love.

Husbands and wives should have all three loves for each other. Your children should see your love. It should be displayed in the warm way you act toward each other—tender words and behavior, affectionate hugs and kisses, special gifts.

**FOUR Ingredients that should be part of a married couple's <u>Romantic Love</u>:**

**1. Desire to be with each other**

- Husbands and wives should eagerly anticipate having time together.
- David B. Webster in his little book, <u>To Love and To Cherish</u>, wrote: "Time spent together is never wasted."
- This desire to spend time together can be lost.
- If you find you are missing this ingredient, find ways to put it back.

**2. Concern for each other's well being**

- Husbands and wives should feel each other's joys and discomforts.
- They should take care to protect and comfort each other.

**3. Strong physical attraction for each other**

- Husbands and wives should be attracted to one another visually and by the sound of their voices and, of course, sexually.

**4. Idealization**

- This means that you see (good) things in each other that others don't see.

John Shoen, a missionary, was speaking to a small group of servicemen and their wives in Japan. Mr. Shoen passed around a small picture of his wife, and said, "I am married to the most beautiful woman in the world."

The young servicemen and their wives nodded politely as they glanced at the picture of the middle-aged woman and passed it along.

Again, Mr. Shoen said, " I am married to the most beautiful woman in the world." Again there was polite silence.

Finally, he said, "I am married to the most beautiful woman in the world . . . because she is my wife."

- Idealization is needed for a good marriage to start, but it continues to be needed in a marriage throughout the years.

If any of these ingredients of Romantic love begins to dwindle away in your Christian marriage—you need to work on "re-installing" the missing ingredient.

A couple needs all four of these ingredients.

## PLACE THE LORD AT THE CENTER OF YOUR LOVE

Do you have a Bible? Do you have a systematic way of daily Bible reading? If not, here is a simple method of daily reading a portion of God's Word, a simple method for people who may not be avid readers:

Read the Gospel of Mark. It is the shortest of the four Gospels, Matthew, Mark, Luke, and John. Try reading through it this way:

**Day One**: read the first four verses of Mark, chapter one. (Mark 1:1-4)

**Day Two**: again read the first four verses of Mark 1, and read the next four verses. (Mark 1:1-8)

**Each succeeding day**, read the last four verses you read the day before, and then next four verses.

It will look like this:

Monday – Mark 1:1-4

Tuesday – Mark 1:1-8

Wednesday – Mark 1:5-12

Thursday – Mark 1:9-16

Friday – Mark 1:13-20

Saturday – Mark 1:17-24, and so on.

It will not take you much time each day. It will not take you many days to read through the Gospel of Mark, and when you complete the Gospel of Mark, you will have read it twice.

Then you can go to another part of the Bible (First John, for instance), and use the same method. Why, you could read the entire Bible that way!

**Learn to pray together**. I have found that consistently praying together is one of the most difficult things for most couples to do. Maybe it is because of busy schedules, or a natural (but not godly) spiritual shyness. I don't know.

But if you need help with this, let me offer you a simple way. Perhaps something like this:

At breakfast each day (or, if you don't eat breakfast, set aside a few minutes before you go your separate ways), take two minutes to do one of four things:

> - **Praise/Adoration** – a sentence praising the Lord for something that causes you wonder—His love for you, His Creation, Marriage, Music, etc.
> - **Confession of sin** – Each of you confess to the Lord some way that you know you are not pleasing Him.
> - **Ask** – Often we think of things that we desire that God alone can provide: wisdom, health, children, spiritual maturity, etc.
> - **Thanksgiving** – Thank the Lord for the family He has made of you, the health to go to work, your salvation, the income He has given you to work with, etc.

Each subsequent day, choose another of these four things. Rotate through them regularly.

Praying together for two minutes a day is better than not praying together at all.

The Bible tells us it is extremely important to the Lord that we, as married couples, attend a Bible-teaching Church regularly.

**Hebrews 10:25 (TLB)** *Let us not neglect our church meetings, as some people do, but encourage and warn each other, especially now that the day of His coming back again is drawing near.*

It is important, not only to attend a Bible-teaching church regularly, but in addition, to build Christian friendships and involve yourselves in your local church by using your talents and giftedness to help in church ministry.

## SESSION 3: LET'S COMMUNICATE

In marriage, communicating well can be a great joy and adventure. Communicating poorly (or not at all) can bring great disappointment into your marriage. A good way to observe your understanding of interpersonal communication necessary in marriage is to ask yourselves these questions and give yourselves time to think and answer them.

Ask yourselves and discuss between you the following questions:

**What improves in your marriages if you are communicating together well?**

Some possible answers:
- o   Problem-solving;
- o   child-rearing;
- o   romance;
- o   dealing with sorrow or trouble;
- o   spiritual-growth;
- o   health;
- o   joy and adventure in life; etc.

**What are some causes of poor communications in marriage?**

Possible answers:

1. Busy-ness
2. Being Tired
3. Family tendency to develop different interests
4. Interference of relatives
5. Basic differences in opinions, in backgrounds, etc.
6. Not listening
7. Not talking

**What are some results of poor communication in marriage?**

Possible answers:

1. Misunderstandings
2. Unhappiness
3. Mistrust
4. New companionships (who provide better communication)
5. Drifting into alcoholism, drugs

In order to defend against communication problems becoming major conflicts within your marriage, it is important to remember that *your marriage is more important* than either of you getting your own way or winning an argument.

**In the event communication conflicts begin to develop, . . .**

## HERE ARE SOME COMMUNICATION-CONFLICT "CURATIVES"

- **Love the Lord. Trust fully in Him.**
    a. Anticipate that _there will be times of conflict_ between any two people.
    b. Meditate on Matthew 6:25-34 - seeking how to keep the first things first, and how simply good is the life God has given you.
    c. Prepare your attitudes and responses ahead of time for conflicts when they arise. "How am I going to act? Or react? How can I control my emotions rather than having my emotions control me, and my words, and my face?"
        - Practice kind attitudes, actions, and responses at home, at work, and at church.
    d. Determine together, and individually, that you will NOT give up on one another—even when you may feel hurt.
        - Remind yourself often that _your marriage is more important than either of you getting your own way or winning in a disagreement._

107

e.  Force yourself to *enter back into loving communication,* sacrificially . . . even when you think your spouse should be the one to "go first."

-   **Love each other. Trust each other.**

    a.  Go back again and *review 1 Corinthians 13:4-8,* God's list of ways that love behaves.

    b.  *Practice* that passage every day of your marriage.

    c.  *Work hard* at your love—every day.

**SOME SEED CAUSES OF CONFLICT**:

It is very easy to begin to believe that you have certain "rights" you expect from your marriage partner. It is easy to insist on total control over some possession or place or time. It is easy to expect to develop a mental picture of how you should be treated by your marriage partner.

-   Continue to remind yourself that your marriage is more important than either of you getting your own way or winning an argument.

-   It is better—when considering your rights or possessions or expectations—to pack them up and give them to the Lord.

-   "Lord, You deserved to be treated better than You were, but You gave up those expectations because of Your love for us. If I am never treated as I hoped or expected to be treated by my husband (my wife), I

108

give You those hopes and expectations because of my love of my husband (my wife)."

**SOLUTION**: **Luke 9:23-25** *Then He said to them all, "If anyone desires to come after Me, let him . . .*

1. *deny himself, and*
2. *take up his cross*
3. *daily,*
4. *and follow Me.* $24$*For whoever desires to save his life will lose it, but whoever loses his life for My sake will save it.* $25$*For what profit is it to a man if he gains the whole world, and is himself destroyed or lost?*

- Give all those rights, possessions, and expectations to the Lord.
- If you receive them back through your spouse— wonderful!
- If your spouse forgets (or is not sensitive enough) to treat you as you have the right to be treated, remind the Lord, "That's OK. I gave you my rights anyway. I still love him (her.)"
- **Surrender your marriage to the Lord**. It's His anyway, designed to honor Him. Commit yourself to honor Him in all you do in marriage.

- **In your marriage, with all of your energy, every day, give to your spouse every kindness and benefit that you can imagine.**
    a.  Make your spouse the most important person in your earthly life.
    b.  Go to the Lord and pray for your spouse each day.
    c.  When working to resolve conflict, if your first attempt doesn't solve the problem, keep trying.
    d.  If you quit trying, start again.
    e.  Always start one more time than you quit.
    f.  Your marriage is more important than either of you getting your own way or winning in a disagreement.

### SESSION 4: FINANCES

Finances is one of several common areas of disagreement in marriages. Considering what the Bible says about priorities in handling your money is important to a sound financial plan in your marriage.

### WHAT DO YOU KNOW ABOUT TITHING?

Tithing is commanded in the Old Testament. Tithing means to give ten-percent of your income to the Lord.

**Malachi 3:10 (TLB)**

*"Bring all the tithes into the storehouse so there will be enough food in my Temple. If you do," says the Lord Almighty, "I will open the windows of heaven for you. I will pour out a blessing so great you won't have enough room to take it in! Try it! Let me prove it to you!"*

A pastor friend, Phil Cleigh, said, "This is the only commandment in the Bible that I know of, where God makes a promise and challenges us to *prove Him* by obeying it."

My friend might be right. I haven't found another commandment like that.

I have heard people say that the New Testament does not teach tithing. But Jesus clearly taught tithing in Matthew 23:23. He was scolding some of the religious leaders of His day for getting their priorities wrong. He said to them, in Matthew 23:23 (NLT): *"How terrible it will be for you teachers of religious law and you Pharisees. Hypocrites!*

*For you are careful to tithe even the tiniest part of your income, but you ignore the important things of the law— justice, mercy, and faith. **You should tithe, yes, but you should not leave undone the more important things**.*

- My understanding is that the Bible teaches that a Christian should immediately give 10% of all that God gives to him to his local church. (Malachi 3:10, Matthew 23:23)
- Then he should give an offering from the 90% which remains.
- Christians should trust the Lord that they can live on the balance.
- Having said that, I know that my faith was small when I began to give to the Lord.
- Some of you may face the same problem.
- We will talk about that in a minute, but first let me give you some thoughts on tithing.

## A. Tithing

**SHORT VERSION:** (Here is a plan that works)

1. **Give** 10% (or more) to the local church.
2. **Save** 10% (or more) - for "retirement" or appliances, repairs, etc.
3. **Learn** to live on 70% of your income

## NOW LET'S FLESH THIS PLAN OUT

1. **Give 10% (or more) to the local church.** - That is biblical teaching.

112

It also makes sense to give to your local church where you are being spiritually fed. After all, you pay the restaurant where you eat, you don't eat at McDonalds and then send your payment to another restaurant that you think needs the money more than McDonalds.

**2. Save 10% (or more)** - The Bible speaks of being wise in handling money, storing up for the future, being generous with money, and taking care not to depend upon, or love, money.[1]

**Invest for retirement.** Be wise. Seek the advice of financial counselors who believe the Bible gives good direction for handing money.

**Save for purchases** (appliances, cars, etc.). It seems to me better to buy only when you have the money. In buying a home, for example, save while you are renting an apartment, until you have enough cash saved to purchase a home, and then consider whether the house that you want is a good purchase and whether you want to exhaust your savings to buy it. Or ask your financial counselor, "Would it be prudent to take out a mortgage ('rent' the bank's money) while our savings continues earning interest?"

---

[1] Proverbs 3:9-10; 6:6-8; 13:16; 16:2; 21:20; Eccl. 11:2; Matthew 6:25-34; 25:14-30; 1 Timothy 6:17, for a few examples.    See also Appendix #5

Another example of "saving to buy" would be to buy cars with cash and keep them in good repair. I don't know who told me, "The cheapest car is the one you own," but it has been a good plan for us.

Another source I read said the best deal on buying cars is to buy a 10-year-old car, drive it for five years, then buy another 10-year-old car.

In any case, it is financially prudent to save and buy when you have the money rather than buying on credit.

### 3. Learn to live on 70% of your income
- Plan
- Set and keep Goals
- Practice financial Discipline

Maybe you think, "Your 'Short Version' of a financial plan only adds up to 90%."

You're right. The other 10% serves as a cushion, a buffer. From this you can give an offering, you can build an emergency fund, save for buying gifts, etc. There may even be a necessary expense that you forgot to calculate in your budget.

This simple plan is a place to start. It's better to start somewhere than not to start at all.

Build your plan and work your plan. Start where your faith is, then stretch your faith. If you cannot make ends meet at any point, make an appointment with a trusted financial counselor, or a church leader or a pastor for help.

But don't give up your determination to obey the Lord in this matter.

Now let's talk about the difficulty that some of us have with building a money plan, and how to include giving, even tithing, in that plan. As I mentioned before, my faith was small when I began to give to the Lord.

Here's my suggestion:
- Begin to tithe what you have faith to tithe—what you can *cheerfully* give to the Lord.

**2 Corinthians 9:7 (NIV)** *Each man should give what he has decided in his heart to give, not reluctantly or under compulsion, for God loves a cheerful giver.*

The Lord loves a *cheerful* giver. What can you give *cheerfully* to the Lord? Can you *cheerfully* give to the Lord 10% of your Gross Income?
- . . . your Gross after taxes?
- . . . your Take-home pay?
- . . . your Take-home after taxes?
- . . . your Take-home after taxes & mortgage?

Whatever 10% you decide that you can *cheerfully* give to the Lord, tithe something! And do it consistently.

Then:

- Set a goal for next month, or next year
- Continue to grow in your faith and giving
- When you have reached the goal of tithing your gross income,

    add a "giving-goal" to your tithes,

    and watch God provide the increase.

**2 Corinthians 9:12-13 (TLB)** *So two good things happen as a result of your gifts—those in need are helped, and they overflow with thanks to God.*

*13 Those you help will be glad not only because of your generous gifts to themselves and to others, but they will praise God for this proof that your deeds are as good as your doctrine.*


Sometimes people ask, **Where should my giving go?**

- I know of no neat breakdown in Scripture that tells us how to divide your giving to support the many worthy ministries serving the Lord.

I have already suggested that the first 10% should go to the local church—after that, I would suggest . . .

- Something to Missions

    Something more to outside ministries

- A goal of tithes and offerings equal to 20%

## B. **Checking accounts**

Keep your financial records balanced.

Which of you can do that better? He, or she, should keep the books.

Work together. Learn how to improve.

Don't grow impatient with your plan or with each other.

One joint checking account should be accessible to both of you.

## C. **Budget**

We should have financial standards and a plan for using God's monetary gifts which He entrusts to us. Here are some of my suggestions:

Problems develop with spending, not with earning:

- Determine together to live within your incomes.
- Both of you should have a small pocket allowance.
- Grocery money should be a regular amount.
- The "grocery shopper" in your marriage should have full freedom to spend the grocery amount decided.
- Remember: You are teammates, not competitors.

117

- Resist salesmen and sales pressure.
- General Rule: You cannot afford to buy things from people who come to your home trying to sell you their product.
- The internet has become a competitive marketplace. If you do internet shopping you need to be careful that you are not seduced by sales pressure.
- You need to be *prayerfully*-involved in the marketplace (stores, Mall, Internet):
  o Decide what you are going to buy, save for it, then go and find the best buy. (Cheapest is not always best.)

**D.** **Threats to budget** – Can you name some threats to a budget?

Here are some budget threats you might consider

- **Homes or apartments that are too expensive.** **One Guideline** suggests that you spend no more than half of our <u>net income</u> on housing, including utilities.

- The latest **electronic equipment**, gadgets, or "time-saving devices."

- New **cars** (and many used cars) are beyond the range for many married couples.

- **Credit cards** – If you use them, pay them off each month. Have the money available before you "charge it." Don't buy much on credit.

118

Think of your marriage as a lifelong adventure together to meet your financial needs and stay within your budget. Keep your credit rating good. Pay all your bills ahead of time.

## E. Gambling

    - **Gambling** is NOT "gaming"

    - True "gaming" would give you a fifty-fifty chance to win by your skill

       -   We would simply discourage *any gambling* for reasons we have included at the end of this book in a <u>Scripture Study concerning Gambling.</u> (Appendix #6)

## SESSION 5: HEALTH, SEXUALITY, INTERPERSONAL RELATIONSHIPS

### HEALTH

Personal Health is a responsibility of the husband for his wife, and of the wife for her husband.

**1 Corinthians 7:4** *The wife does not have authority over her own body, but the husband does. And likewise the husband does not have authority over his own body, but the wife does.*

### Agree together to eat nutritiously.

There are many opinions of how healthy and how nutritious Healthy-Nutritious eating is. Learn together. Agree together. Change your opinions when you can do it in agreement.

Here's a simple plan:

Eat fruits, vegetables, grains, and small meat portions.

Drink a lot of water.

Be careful with snack foods and desserts.

### Allow enough time in your schedule for sleep

This is hard for many couples. But determine together you are going to invest in some exercise each day. Then do it. Walking, going to the Y or a gym, whatever works best for both of you.

- Go to your Doctor for annual physicals and discuss any medical problems together and with your health care provider.

## YOUR SEXUAL RELATIONSHIP

I want to talk with you frankly about ways of keeping your intimate life fresh throughout your marriage. An unscriptural sexual relationship can be an area of problems in marriage.

**1 Corinthians 7:2-5 (NIV)** *But since there is so much immorality, each man should have his own wife, and each woman her own husband.*

*3 The husband should fulfill his marital duty to his wife, and likewise the wife to her husband. 4 The wife's body does not belong to her alone but also to her husband. In the same way, the husband's body does not belong to him alone but also to his wife. 5 Do not deprive each other except by mutual consent and for a time, so that you may devote yourselves to prayer. Then come together again so that Satan will not tempt you because of your lack of self-control.*

Husbands and wives are stewards of each other's bodies—to protect, care for, love, and treat with respect. Sexual behavior is an important God-given discipline and joy for married couples.

121

Here are some important principles for intimacy in a Christian marriage:

### 1. Personal purity

**Don't toy with sexual discipline.**

Determine to avoid flirting with anyone other than your spouse.

Avoid immoral or sexually-suggestive entertainment, perversions, pornographic materials or imaginations.

Keep your imagination pure—only for marriage— only for each other.

If there are problems in your sexual discipline, solve them.

**2. Sexual intimacy** is an important part of godly marriage. Be faithful to each other sexually and emotionally and in your imagination.

**Proverbs 5:18 (NIV)** *May your fountain be blessed, and may you **rejoice in the wife of your youth**.*

a. Sexual intimacy is God's seal upon a godly marriage.

**Genesis 2:24** *Therefore a man shall leave his father and mother and be joined to his wife, and they shall become one flesh.*

b. Sex is not a subject for jokes or entertainment.

c. Sexual intimacy is a sacred act of marital unity – a tender event; a joyful event; a private event. A covenant from God. (Genesis 2:24, Matthew 19:4-5, Ephesians 5:31)

- When there are children in the home, be sure to keep a lock on your bedroom door.

Normally, sex is a very simple thing. A man is easily aroused—visually, with words, perfume, and with memories. So build good memories together.

A woman may or may not be so easily aroused. Before sexual relations begin, a wife normally needs to feel emotionally security and sense that she can trust her husband. Her husband needs to behave in a <u>genuinely loving way</u> toward his wife.

Review the behaviors of love in 1 Corinthians 13:4-8 (pp. 88-94). It's a husband's privilege and joy to provide emotional security and genuine love to his wife.

- In a godly marriage, sexual satisfaction of your mate should be the concern for each of you.
- Because the husband is easier to satisfy, he has to take extra care to learn what pleases his wife.
- It is okay to ask each other throughout your years of marriage what is pleasurable and what is not.
- It is helpful to study a book together that talks about the godly physical relationship within marriage. For example: "INTENDED FOR PLEASURE" by Dr. Ed Wheat and Gaye Wheat
- Be careful what you watch (TV, movies, computer) and listen to, and be careful what you meditate on.
- Stay away from pornography, pornographic thinking, fanaticizing about intimacy with others

123

outside your marriage, or flirting with anyone except your spouse.

- Sex should never be used as a weapon or bargaining chip.
- If any of the above sinful habits have been part of your life, confess it to the Lord, ask Him to take away those memories and thoughts, and work at replacing those thoughts with Philippians 4:8 kinds of thinking.

**Philippians 4:8** *Finally, brethren, whatever things are true, whatever things are noble, whatever things are just, whatever things are pure, whatever things are lovely, whatever things are of good report, if there is any virtue and if there is anything praiseworthy--meditate on these things.*

- Over the years of your marriage be aware that emotional and physical changes may take place that may affect intimacy.
- If a time comes when through illness or injury or for other reasons sexual relations are not possible, your marriage should be strong enough emotionally and spiritually to continue to strengthen in spite of the loss. Remain faithful to the Lord and to each other.

### 3. Birth control

- There are **many kinds of birth control** available, if you choose to use them.
    - Condoms are convenient and easy to use.
    - When purchasing condoms, look for lubricated styles.
    - It is also good to have a water-soluble lubricant in your bedroom, such as "K-Y Jelly" (or liquid)
    - Birth control pills: Discuss side effects with a doctor before you use them.


- What about **permanent birth control**?
    - Agree together if you are considering a permanent pregnancy-preventative measure.
    - Make your choice a matter of prayer and make your choice subject to the leading of the Lord.
    - Honor one another
    - Determine not to blame each other if you agree and make a permanent change, then later regret that decision.

- It is very easy for most women to become pregnant.

125

- Birth control should be planned ahead, kept convenient.
- **God does not allow for abortion (Psalm 139:13-16)**
- An unplanned child will be loved as much as a planned one.

**4. For older couples—or second marriages:**

a. Deal honestly and openly about your first marriage(s).

b. Put away fantasies about other relationships outside marriage.

c. Be faithful to each other.

d. Develop your "best friendship" with one another.

## INTERPERSONAL AND SOCIAL RELATIONSHIPS

Work hard together to make your social friendships good.

Don't make fun of your spouse in public or to your friends.

When you are with family members or friends, don't tell stories about your spouse in a funny way. (Unless you have explicit permission from your spouse to tell the story)

Don't solve problems after 10 pm. If there is a "deadlock disagreement" and you are both weary of trying to find a resolution, make an appointment to take up the discussion the next day, then get a good night's rest.

Make allowance in your communication together for the fact that we are all subject to cycles of emotion—some of us more than others.

Be sensitive and gentle with each other.

Care for one another's health and eating habits.

Work to maintain positive attitudes in your marriage.

Communicate openly on many subjects. Learn to listen.

Develop each other's strengths.

Don't try to change each other. (Even if you notice areas you would *like* to change.) Admire each other. Accept your spouse as he or she is. Allow your spouse to be different than you are, to hold different opinions, to be the individual God has made him to be.

Build each other. Work hard, together, to make good relationships with other people.

## GETTING ALONG WITH FAMILY

It may not have occurred to you that when you married you brought your two families together.

Work hard TOGETHER to get along with both of your families.

It is more important that you learn to understand your extended family (including your in-laws) than it is that they understand you.

Plan visits to both families regularly, at least at holiday times. Plan always to go TOGETHER to visit family. When you left your parents and became a married couple, your families felt the loss to a greater or a lesser degree. You need your family independence, but be gracious. Make your marriage a gain for your families.

If there are social, ethnic, or religious differences between your families, or between you and your families, work hard to understand, and to be hospitable.

You can be sacrificial. Remember, the Lord gave His life for you.

## CHURCH LIFE

Don't forget the Lord in your marriage. _Make a habit of regular church attendance._ You should not have to decide _if_ you are going to go to church. Make it your habit that on Sunday, as a family, you will be at church—on time. Your children will adopt your habit.

Develop a schedule that will get you to church early. Christian author Henrietta Mears said, "If you're not ten minutes early, you're late."

Pastor's wife and author Anne Ortland wrote, "The idea is to express eagerness. If you stand around yakking outside, you give off the aroma that you consider meeting people more important than meeting God."

Become involved in ministering together with your church family. Get to know your church family well.

## PERSONAL DEVOTIONAL LIFE

Read the Scripture and pray together at least once a week.

Make this a permanent part of your marriage. Restart as often as is necessary. It may be helpful to have a Bible at your dining room table. Before you eat breakfast (or any meal) read a short portion of scripture and pray.

Each of you individually needs to have time for personal devotions every day, too. Start small if you need to, and grow in this habit.

## ROMANCE

Make romance a regular part of your schedule. Keep dating each other.

Don't allow money to be an issue. There are ways to have dates that cost little or nothing. Ask other married friends what they do for dates.

Keep times guarded to use for dates.

In your home select reading, music, television and other entertainment which honor God, honor marriage, honor the creative mind God gave you, and honor the romance that keeps your marriage fresh.

## PREVENTATIVE COUNSELING

Invite your pastor and his wife into your home from time to time to share with them the joys and surprises of your marriage.

Remember, you can call your pastor any time.

It is always better to visit with your pastor before problems grow serious.

## SESSION 6: CONTROLLING ANGER

What does the Bible say about anger?

In **Ephesians 4:26** the Bible says three things about being angry.

### 1. BE <u>ANGRY</u>

What is anger?

> ANSWER: Anger is an "emotion." The word "emotion" is two words glued together: "**e**" meaning 'to,' plus "**motion**" meaning '**move**." An emotion is designed *to move* us.

- Anger itself is not a sin. It is a God-given, powerful motivator.

- VINCENT'S Word Studies of the New Testament say: *"Righteous anger is commanded; not merely permitted."*

- Anger has its place as a motivator for good.

- BUT because anger is so powerful, it is also dangerous.

- AND anger *should not* become a habit—

> But only an <u>occasional incident</u>—

> > Kept under control—

> > > driving you to do good.

The second thing **Ephesians 4:26** says about anger:

### 2. DO NOT <u>SIN</u>

- When we are angry, we have a choice:

> to act sinfully, or

> to act without sinning.

131

- Our natural (human) inclination when we are angry is to react sinfully, but instead . . .
- Remember the Lord.
- Imitate the Lord.
- When does anger turn to sin?
- POSSIBLE ANSWERS:
  When we brood against someone who has wronged us.
  When we create and hold grudges.
  When we continue to rehearse the hurt someone has caused us.
- When our anger *does* turn to sin, as with any other sin, we must confess our sin and turn away (repent) from it.
- **1 John 1:9** *If we confess our sins, He is faithful and just to forgive us our sins and to cleanse us from all unrighteousness.*

  **Acts 3:19** *Repent therefore and be converted, that your sins may be blotted out, so that times of refreshing may come from the presence of the Lord,*

The third thing **Ephesians 4:26** says about anger:
### 3. DO NOT LET THE SUN GO DOWN ON YOUR WRATH.
- This phrase is telling us how seriously God expects us to handle anger in our lives.

- Deal with anger concretely, definitely, resolutely, decisively, absolutely and "in no uncertain terms."
- Deal with anger quickly, immediately.

Anger is a God-given motivator you want to use quickly and correctly, to do good, to be constructive, then dispose of it quickly.

Anger is like a lit stick of dynamite in your hand. You need to decide quickly what to do with your anger and do <u>what is right</u>. Do it <u>quickly</u>, before it explodes and becomes destructive.


There is only one place I *know* where the Bible specifically says that Jesus was angry. We find that in **Mark 3:1-5**.

In other passages we read that Jesus overturned the tables of the money-changers in the temple. (**John 2:13-17**) He *may* have been angry then, but the Bible doesn't specifically say so. At the time of that incident, Jesus' disciples remembered an Old Testament quotation, **Psalm 69:9** *Because zeal for Your house has eaten me up, . . .*

*Zeal* is another word for emotion. Jesus had apparently shown strong emotion. That emotion might have been anger. Or, it might have been sorrow, disappointment, or some other strong emotion. We are not told.

But in **Mark 3:1-5** we know for sure Jesus was angry, because the Bible tells us so. Look in your Bibles and read the passage in Mark 3:1-5.

"What three things did Jesus DO with His anger?" (Mark 3:5)

Give yourself a few minutes to discover those three things. Below are some answers if you need them.

Answer: In His anger, Jesus . . .

v. 5 – . . . "<u>looked around</u> at his enemies" (Was that sinful?)

- . . . "<u>grieved</u>" for His enemies (Was that sinful?)
- . . . <u>healed</u> the man with the crippled hand (Was that sinful?)

Jesus was angry. But He did not sin in His anger. He did not let the sun go down on His anger. He used His anger to do good; and He did it quickly.

Ask yourself, *What can I do when I am angry that is NOT sin?*

For instance, what can you do (that is not sinful) when you hit your thumb with a hammer?

SOME POSSIBLE ANSWERS, when you need suggestions:

<u>Change</u> your hammering technique

<u>Practice</u> to improve hand-eye coordination

<u>Go</u> to the hospital for treatment

"Are those things sinful?"

134

What can you do when a fellow-employee criticizes your work?

Possible answers:

Examine your work: "Is my critic right? partly-right? or wrong?"

From time to time a pastor may get comments or notes about how to be a better pastor. If he considers the comment, the pastor can usually discover something that helps him, once he gets over his self-pity.

Examine your relationship with that fellow-employee: Have you been Christ-like toward him?

Can you be a better friend to him?

Is there something he needs? Is he crying out for your help?

Is there something you can do to help your fellow-employee be less critical and more productive?


What can you do when a family member does not treat you right? (Husband, wife, child, parent, etc.)

Possible answers:

Forgive him or her

Examine *your role* in the family as a husband (or wife, or father, or mother, or child)

Study to learn what God's Word says about the way a (husband, wife, parent, child) should live?

When you become angry, try to quickly remember that anger is a God-given motivator to do good. But, as a motivator, anger must be handled quickly and correctly.

**There is something else the Bible says about Anger** that emphasizes the importance of taking care of that emotion quickly and correctly.

**Ephesians 4:31** *Let all bitterness, wrath, anger, clamor, and evil speaking be put away from you, with all malice.*

Here God shows us . . .

**A Progressive Development of anger which needs to be broken** as early as possible:

**BITTERNESS** - internal, acidy frame of mind

**WRATH** - quick temper, short fuse

**ANGER** - enduring, violent outward expression

**CLAMOR** - loud quarreling

**EVIL - SPEAKING** - abusive, hate-filled speech, cursing and worse (blasphemy)

**MALICE** - vicious, evil intentions

You will notice the destructive progression in this list, from milder to more severe forms of anger. You may discover yourself in this progressive list. The key is to break this chain as early as possible.

In prison visits I have made, I have often noticed that inmates are incarcerated because they have allowed

136

this progression to develop until, in violent anger, they did what they should not have done.

Social groups, media, military training, gangs, political gatherings, even athletic teams or coaches will sometimes *encourage* progressive anger or rage to motivate their members.

It might work in combative competition, but it is not biblical. It does not work well in marriage and family relationships.


When you become angry, try to quickly remember that anger is a God-given motivator to do good.

Take control of your anger. Don't let it take control of you.

Use it to do good. Do so quickly and correctly.

Then be rid of the anger.

Don't brood over wrong done to you.

Don't hold a grudge.

Don't even remember it. God says, **Hebrews 10:17** . . . *"Their sins and their lawless deeds I will remember no more."*

God chooses not to remember the sins of those who have confessed their sins to him and forsaken them. God is the Example we need to follow when someone wrongs us. In your anger do good, and do it quickly.

Then determine not to remember the sins others have committed against you.

Don't meditate on them.

137

Don't re-enact or rehearse the hurt.

Don't recite it to others.

Forgive. Put it out of your memory. Choose not to rehearse it, repeat it, or think about it.

Sometimes that takes God's help. Ask Him for it, and then do it.

## SESSION 7: DEALING WITH CONFLICT IN MARRIAGE

Conflicts are inevitable in human relationships. Marriage is no exception. Thank the Lord for His Word with which He directs us what to do in times of conflict.

Thank Him for His Holy Spirit to enable us, as followers of Jesus, to do right when conflict arises.

In Scriptures which teach us how to resolve conflict, an important principle to observe is this:

### THE AIM IS ALWAYS RECONCILIATION

The purpose of biblical counseling is to lay a strong foundation for your marriage. A marriage foundation to last a lifetime.

Recognize that anything that you do in Christ's name as you deal with conflict between yourself and anyone else (including family members) needs to be a **ministry of reconciliation**.

In a Christian marriage if the conflict becomes so dangerous that there is need for a physical separation—that separation is for safety and for time to figure out a way to reconcile. It is not intended to be a time to try a new freedom from marriage.

**The aim is always reconciliation.**

Divorce is never commanded in the Scripture and is permitted only for unfaithfulness or habitual immorality. It is a last resort for the sorrowful end of a long series of failed efforts to reconcile.

In **Matthew 18:15-20**, the Lord gives us a plan for reconciling conflicts that can be applied to conflicts within marriage.

## A MINISTRY OF RECONCILIATIONS IN MARRIAGE
**2 Corinthians 5:20**

*We are therefore Christ's ambassadors, as though God were making his appeal through us. We implore you on Christ's behalf: <u>Be reconciled</u> to God.*

If a husband and a wife are reconciled to God, they will find ways of reconciling with each other.

Jesus' instructions for reconciling a conflict between a married Christian couple are clearly and simply given in **Matthew 18:15-20**:

*"If your brother sins against you, go and show him his fault, just between the two of you. If he listens to you, you have won your brother over. [16]But if he will not listen, take one or two others along, so that 'every matter may be established by the testimony of two or three witnesses.' [17]If he refuses to listen to them, tell it to the church; and if he refuses to listen even to the church, treat him as you would a pagan or a tax collector.*

*[18]"I tell you the truth, whatever you bind on earth will be bound in heaven, and whatever you loose on earth will be loosed in heaven.*

[19]*"Again, I tell you that if two of you on earth agree about anything you ask for, it will be done for you by my Father in heaven.* [20]*For where two or three come together in my name, there am I with them."*

1. **The first step of reconciliation is for the offended party to go to the offender privately and try to agree together.**

   **Matthew 18:15** *Moreover if your brother sins against you, go and tell him his fault between you and him alone. If he hears you, you have gained your brother.*

   If this first step is handled biblically, many conflicts are resolved. If not, the conflicts can grow worse.

   a. *"between you and him alone"* – Keep the "circle" small. In marriage conflict, keep it between husband and wife, if possible. There is a great temptation to share the problem with close friends or family members. Try to NOT do that.

   If it has already been shared, when the conflict is reconciled, you will have the added problem of going to those you have told and try to undo bad feelings that might have developed.

141

b. A large percentage of conflicts between Christian husbands and wives will be resolved in this first step as the couple works through their disagreements and conflicts.

c. Don't brood or build a grudge. Don't entertain thoughts of revenge. *"Go and tell him his fault between you and him alone."*

d. Carefully craft the language and the attitudes you will use when you go to talk with your spouse, remembering that <u>the aim is always reconciliation</u>.

If the conflict continues, then proceed to the second step:

2. **The second step is for the offended party to take one or two others with him to the offender and together try to reconcile.**

a. This is an instruction to seek help from one or two godly counselors. **Matthew 18:16** *But if he will not hear, take with you one or two more, that 'by the mouth of two or three witnesses every word may be established.'*

b. The selection of the *"one of two others"* should be people that both you and your spouse respect, trust, and admire.

c. I have often thought that Jesus, in His fore-wisdom was implying that the *"one or two others,"* might be older, godly, married friends who have a good marriage; perhaps

142

your pastor and his wife; or marriage counselors that have a strong, Christ-centered marriage.

d. In any case, these "*one or two others*" need to be strong believers in Bible teaching for marriage.

e. Notice the "circle" of involvement is still being kept small.

f. Never forget, <u>the aim is always reconciliation.</u>

## 3. The third step is to take the matter to the church

### Matthew 18:17a

*And if he refuses to hear them, tell it to the church.*

a. I believe *this does not mean* to gossip it through the church body or to make an announcement in a church service or in a venue for prayer requests.

b. I believe that Jesus refers here to the leadership of the church, to the pastor and the elders (deacons), appealing to the elders (deacons) for help to reconcile the disagreement or offence.

c. This instruction is for husband and wife both to submit to church leadership for help, for biblical instruction.

143

d.   The church leaders might counsel the husband and wife concerning their financial situation. Finances are a leading cause of marriage conflict. Or, they may do some anger-management counseling. Or, send the couple to a marriage retreat (Fairhaven Ministries in Tennessee, for example). Or something else.

e.   Keep remembering, <u>the aim is always reconciliation</u>.

4.   **Finally, if the problem is not resolved by these first 3 steps, Jesus says in Matthew 15:17b . . .** *But if he refuses even to hear the church, let him be to you like a heathen and a tax collector.*

a.   Does that sound harsh and "un-Jesus-like?"

b.   It might *seem* harsh until you think about Jesus Himself.

c.   Ask: How did Jesus treat heathen and tax collectors?

   i.   Think about that and answer.

   ii.   Jesus *loved* "heathen and tax collectors." He consistently tried to woo them into His Kingdom. His love for them took Jesus to the Cross.

d.   The Aim is Always Reconciliation.

e.   This instruction means that the resolution of this conflict, having reached this point, might

144

require *a long, faithful journey,* loving an offending spouse and doing all possible, even sacrificially, to win him (her) back.

f.   I have known marriages where one spouse becomes a Christian, but the other spouse resists spiritual commitment to Jesus. I have seen that Christian spouse faithfully love and, in a Christ-like manner, do everything possible to win the marriage-mate to the Lord. For years.

g.   This step means that in an un-reconciled conflict, the Christian spouse (and they may both be Christians, even if they are in conflict) needs to treat the other as Jesus would treat a non-believer, lovingly and patiently trying to win them back.

h.   Notice this example from Jesus' life:

**Matthew 9:10-13** *While Jesus was having dinner at Matthew's house, many tax collectors and sinners came and ate with him and his disciples. [11] When the Pharisees saw this, they asked his disciples, "Why does your teacher eat with tax collectors and 'sinners'?"*

*[12] On hearing this, Jesus said, "It is not the healthy who need a doctor, but the sick. [13] But go and learn what this means: 'I desire mercy, not sacrifice.' For I have not come to call the righteous, but sinners."*

**The aim is always reconciliation**.

(See also Mt. 15:22-28, and Luke 19:1-10)

**Luke 19:10**

*For the Son of Man came to seek and to save what was lost."*

In this instruction, treating your spouse-in-conflict the way Jesus treated "heathen and tax collectors," you have an opportunity to begin a new, strong and long-term ministry in your marriage—a ministry of reconciliation.

5. **The last two verses in this passage instruct you never to quit praying for** (not against) **your husband/wife, even in times of conflict. (Mt. 18:18-19)**

   - In our Christian marriages, we have two objectives to keep in mind as we deal with conflict among us.
   - First, we want to stop any sin in our own lives.
   - Second, we want to reconcile with our spouse.

**A WARNING TO ALL OF US:**

**Galatians 6:1-5**

*Brothers, if someone is caught in a sin, you who are spiritual should restore him gently. But watch yourself, or you also may be tempted. [2]Carry each other's burdens, and in this way you will fulfill the law of Christ. [3]If anyone thinks he is something when he is nothing, he deceives himself.*

[4]Each one should test his own actions. Then he can take pride in himself, without comparing himself to somebody else, [5]for each one should carry his own load.

## A FINAL WORD

Our prayer is that this book might be a useful resource to pastors, marriage counselors, students, young married couples, and couples that are not so young.

Marriage is God's painting. It is His mystery, once hidden, but now revealed in His Word. (Ephesians 3:4-5, 14-20; 5:21-33)

In biblical Christian marriage it is God's intention to display, in human form, a picture of the relationship between the Lord Jesus Christ (the groom) and His bride (the Church—all who have placed their faith in Jesus for everlasting life).

Our world has altered, licensed, distorted, and corrupted God's picture. In so doing, the colors of marriage, the distinct images God intended have been lost to opinions, laws, and careless ignorance.

In the 16th century, Michelangelo painted the ceiling of the Sistine chapel in vivid, colored detail. But over the centuries both the color and detail faded. It was no longer a vivid set of Bible stories in picture.

The 20th century restoration of the Sistine ceiling has, not without controversy, reclaimed Michelangelo's eloquent art for visitors to again observe. The pictures once again tell Bible stories.

A biblical marriage tells the story of God's love for His people and their love for, and submission to, Him. We pray that some of the biblical details in this book will help establish marriages that display God's lovely plan when one man and one woman to come together for a life-long commitment to God and to each other.

For others, whose marriages that may have grown dull, we pray that this book might help restore all the color and vivid detail God intended.

Paul Frederick
Maurice Russell

**APPENDICES:**

These are interesting bits of information that may be helpful for the pastor, or pre-marriage couples, or older, well-established married couples.

## Appendix # 1 – COVENANTS, CONTRACTS, AND TRADITIONS

### A. The Marriage Covenant

Christian marriage is to be a **<u>covenant</u>**—not a **<u>contract</u>**. A **covenant** is a sacred, unconditional, lifetime vow—a permanent promise.

A **contract** is conditional: "If you do this, I will do that. If you break your promise, I am free from my promise, too."

Marriage is a **covenant**, not a **contract**. The marriage **covenant** says, "I am placing my entire faith in you. You can trust me with your life, too. Until death do us part."

A marriage **contract** says, "I'm not sure I can trust you. So if you break this agreement, I am released from this marriage."

## B. Sample "Repeat After Me" Vows

**VOWS:**

I _____ take you _____ to be my wife/husband, to have and to hold, from this day forward, for better for worse, for richer for poorer, in sickness and in health, to love and to cherish, till death do us part. I promise I will be always faithful to you. I will never leave you nor forsake you. These vows I make to you / according to God's holy Word, and thereto I give you my love.

## C. TRADITIONAL MEANINGS WITHIN THE WEDDING CEREMONY

1. **Seating** – illustrates the Old Testament blood covenant (Genesis 15:7-18)
   - An animal sacrifice was divided, and those making the covenant passed between the halves.
   - God made His covenant with Abraham and passed between two halves of a divided sacrificial animal.
   - Covenants are not to be broken

2. **White Runner** – beautiful picture of the marriage couple knowing that they are standing on Holy Ground—in the presence of God.

## 3. Groom enters first

- The first party in the covenant assumes the greater responsibility.
- God and Abraham
- Christ and the Church
- Husband and wife

## 4. Father walking his daughter down the aisle

- "I am responsible for my daughter's purity."
- "I found the best young man for her."
- "I am transferring my affection, authority, and responsibility for her to you, young man."

## 5. White wedding dress

- a symbol of the purity of life and heart which the husband will build in his wife. (Ephesians 5:25-27)—It is appropriate for the groom to pay for the wedding dress.

## 6. Holding hands for vows

- symbol of intermingling of blood of covenant
- In an old custom, two parties would cut small slits in their right hands and as their blood mingled, they would list their assets and liabilities.

## 7. Wedding rings

- symbol of strength, unbroken circles
- Husband and wife give each other their strength.
- Husband will surround wife with protection.
- Jonathan and David made a covenant. Jonathan gave David his belt (symbol of strength – 1 Sam. 18:4), and the promise was that if any should oppose one of them, he opposed them both.
- God gave the circle of the rainbow as a ring symbolizing His protection from future judgment by flood.

## 8. Formal introductions

- Bride takes a new name—that of her husband
- Abram "high father" became Abraham "father of a multitude"—recognizing God's covenant with him.
- First century believers became "Christians"— taking on the name of the Lord.

## 9. Guest book – witnesses to this solemn covenant

## 10. Feeding cake to each other

- "our communion together"
- "Mine is yours. Yours is mine."

## 11. Throwing rice or other seeds

- God gives seed to the marriage.
- Couple is to be fruitful and raise "spiritual trees" from God-blessed seed—Children around God's table.

**APPENDIX # 2 - ORDER OF SERVICE –**

(This is a template from which to plan the ceremony. For each couple, some things will be added, and some deleted, and some rearranged. This template is only intended to be a list of possibilities for the couple to think about in planning their ceremony with the pastor.)

Prelude – 15-20 minutes while guests are seated. –

Ushers: (Who will they be?)

      Groom's grandparents (to right, facing Pastor)

      Bride's grandparents (left)

      Groom's parents (right)

      Bride's mother (left)

Mothers light candles

Aisle runner (Will you use one?)

Pastor and Groom enter from the side

Musicians begin processional

Bridal party enters: (Men on the right/Ladies on the left)

Flower girl and ring bearer (Will you use these?)

Wedding March

*** CONGREGATION STANDS***

Bride and her Father enter

Scripture and prayer
***CONGREGATION SEATED***
Announcement: *In respect to the family, if you have a cell phone or a pager or beeper, would you please turn them off at this time?*

Introductory remarks – Pastor

Vows "I do"

Pastor: "Who gives Bride to be married to Groom?"

Bride's Father,: "Her mother and I do." (or equivalent)
> Groom steps down to meet Bride
> Father places Bride's hand in Groom's
> Father is seated
> Groom and Bride walk hand in hand to Pastor

Special song:

Message (4-8 minutes) – Pastor

Bride gives bouquet to Maid/Matron of Honor

Vows "Repeat after me"

    (If there are creative vows, the pastor will want to go over them with the

        couple well ahead of the wedding date.)

Ring ceremony   (Who will carry the rings?)

Prayer

Special song, while the following take place:

    Communion (This would be just for Bride and Groom, if they want it)

        Unity Candle

        Bride & Groom will give flowers to Moms

Pronouncement –

Kiss

Signing of wedding license (at the table with the Unity Candle)

Pastor congratulates couple

Bride receives flowers from Matron of Honor

Benediction

Presentation

Recessional –

Announcements

"Please remain seated until Groom and Bride come back and

dismiss you."

-   Announce reception
-   Turn cell phones back on

Groom and Bride excuse guests
(Alternatives:

Receiving line, with usher's dismissing guests;

Receiving line at the reception)

**Here is a sample of a prepared service order.**

**ORDER OF SERVICE –**

Prelude – 15-20 minutes while guests are seated. – Grace Pianomeister

Ushers: J.R., Matthew
        Caleb's Gr-parents:
                Grandma and Grandpa Jones  (to right, facing Pastor)
                Grandma and Grandpa Smith  (to right, facing Pastor)
        Kayla's grandmother: Grandma Brown (left)
        Caleb's parents:      Trent & Heather  (right)
        Kayla's mother:       Kim  (left)

Mothers light candles

Pastor and Groom (Caleb) enter from the side

Grace  (pianist) begins processional

Bridal party enters: (Men on the right/Ladies on the left)
| Seth | Patience |
| Christian | Betha |
| Kyle | Sarina |
| Ryan | Michelle |
| Andrew | Gentle |
| Gideon | Erica |

Two Flower girls: Praise & Hosanna

Wedding March
*** CONGREGATION STANDS***

Kayla and her Father, enter

Pastor: **Caleb**, to the husband, the Scriptures say:
**Malachi 2:14-15**

*. . . the LORD is acting as the witness between you and the wife of your youth, . . .. So guard yourself in your spirit, and do not break faith with the wife of your youth.*

> . . . and **Kayla**, to the wife the Scriptures say:

**1 Peter 3:1-4**

*Wives, likewise, be submissive to your own husbands, . . .let your adornment be . . . the hidden person of the heart, with the incorruptible beauty of a gentle and quiet spirit, which is very precious in the sight of God.*

Pastor: A union embodying such ideals is not to be entered into lightly or unadvisedly, but reverently, discreetly, soberly, and in the fear of God. Into such a union you come now to be joined.

Pastor: Prayer
***CONGREGATION SEATED***

Pastor's Announcement: In respect to the family, if you have a cell phone or a pager or beeper, would you please turn them off at this time?

Introductory remarks – Pastor (optional)

Pastor: Caleb, do you take Kayla to be your wife; promising to keep, cherish, and protect her? Will you be her faithful and true husband until the coming of our Lord Jesus Christ, or so long as you both shall live?

Caleb: "I do."

Pastor: Kayla, do you take _Caleb_ to be your husband; promising to love, honor, and pray for him each day? Will you be his faithful and true wife until the return of our Lord Jesus Christ, or so long as you both shall live?

Kayla: "I do."

Pastor: Who gives Kayla to be married to Caleb?

Father of the Bride : "Her mother and I do."
      Caleb steps down to meet Kayla

160

Father of the Bride places Kayla's right hand in
Caleb's right hand
Father of the Bride is seated
Caleb and Kayla walk hand in hand to Pastor

Special song: Ryan "When I Say I Do"

Pastor: **Message: "HOPE"**

**Psalm 71:5 (ESV)**
5 For <u>you, O Lord</u>, are <u>my hope</u>, my trust, O LORD, from my
youth.

HOPE = "Eager Expectation" – often used concerning
Heaven.
-   Knowing something good is coming
-   Eagerly awaiting it.

Your marriage is a touch of heaven on earth.
We all eagerly anticipate. . .
. . . witnessing God's best for you and your family
all the days of your lives.


Your marriage is an opportunity to show God's design to a
world that has not much hope—
-   Doesn't see much in the way of hopeful marriages
-   You show them

See your marriage from God's Perspective
-   What does God intend your marriage to be?
His Word tells you:
-   A picture of His Love for His people
-   And their loving, obedient response to Him

Your marriage has an eternal element to it
-   In your marriage you become one: Spirit, Body,
    Mind
-   That doesn't mean identical—far from it
-   But it does mean United—"complementary"

161

- And it pictures Eternity with Jesus
- With Him forever: Spirit, Body, Mind

That's the HOPE found in a Christ-centered Marriage

Kayla gives bouquet to Erica

Pastor: <u>Caleb</u> and <u>Kayla</u>    FACE EACH OTHER. HOLD HANDS.  REPEAT AFTER ME:

I __Caleb__ take you ___Kayla___ to be my wife, to have and to hold, from this day forward, for better for worse, for richer for poorer, in sickness and in health, to love and to cherish, till death do us part. I promise I will be always faithful to you.  I will never leave you nor forsake you. These vows I make to you / according to God's holy Word, and thereto I give you my love.

I ___Kayla___ take you ___Caleb___ to be my husband, to have and to hold, from this day forward, for better for worse, for richer for poorer, in sickness and in health, to love and to cherish, till death do us part. I promise I will be always faithful to you. I will never leave you nor forsake you.  These vows I make to you / according to God's holy Word, and thereto I give you my love.

Ring ceremony (Gideon & Erica will carry the rings)

Pastor: Caleb, what token do you give in acknowledgment of these vows?

<u>Caleb:</u> This ring.

Pastor: This ring is of gold, and is precious; so let your love for your dear bride be your most cherished earthly possession.

(<u>Caleb</u> places ring on <u>Kayla's</u> hand)

Pastor: And <u>Kayla</u>, what token do you give in acknowledgment of these vows?

Kayla: This ring.

Pastor: This ring is a perfect and unbroken circle, the symbol of eternity. So may your love for your husband be endless.

(Kayla places ring on Caleb's hand)

Pastor: With these emblems of strength and unity, purity and endless devotion, showing how lasting and imperishable is the faith you do now mutually pledge, you do each the other wed and these marriage vows you do here and now forever seal.

Prayer – (Pastor or others selected to pray for the couple)

Special song, Blessing & Mercy & Hannah (piano & harp) while . . .
- Kayla & Caleb light Unity Candle
- Kayla & Caleb give flowers to Moms

Pastor: Inasmuch as you entered into these marriage vows before Christ and these witnesses, having pledged yourselves only for each other, I, by the authority vested in me as a minister of the Word of God and by the laws of this state, pronounce you husband and wife, united in pure and holy bonds of wedlock. Those whom God has joined together, let no man separate.

Pastor: Caleb, you may kiss your bride.

Kayla receives flowers from Erica Lee

Signing of wedding license at the communion table on stage

Pastor congratulates couple

Pastor: Benediction – ". . . Be of good comfort, be of one mind, live in peace; and the God of love and peace will be with you. . . . The grace of the Lord Jesus Christ, and the love of God, and the communion of the Holy Spirit be with you . . . AMEN."                    2 Cor 13:11-14


Pastor's Announcements
        "Please remain seated until the ushers come back and dismiss you."
-        Receiving line in the foyer
-        Announce reception in the Fellowship area
-        Turn cell phones back on
-        Pastor: Announce the Reception and its location

Pastor's Presentation – "It is my privilege to present to you Mr. & Mrs. Caleb Smith."

Recessional – Grace

## APPENDIX #3: A STUDY OF MARITAL SUBMISSION

**A study of Ephesians 5:21-33**—concerning the biblical application of submission within human marriage. Let's look how God's marriage plan is meant to work out—according to God's own Word—the Bible:

### Ephesians 5:21 "<u>submitting</u> yourselves to one another..."

- To submit in the Bible means "to arrange under"
- To discover your "role" and fit into it

When you start a new job, you quickly learn to work together with all the different department heads and other employees.

In a marriage, according to God's Word, a husband has certain responsibilities and a wife has others. In a sense, both husband and wife are "department heads."

To submit to one another means to learn to work together in such a way that each of you improves the other . . . makes the other one look good, successful; confident, cheering each other along life's troubling way.

As an example, a husband needs to honor his wife in her administration of their home . . . **1 Timothy 5:14** *Therefore I desire that the younger widows marry, bear children, manage the house, give no opportunity to the adversary to speak reproachfully.*

Or, if his wife works outside the home (or has a work-at-home job), the husband honors and assists her in

165

the work she does and works with her in balancing out the work of family and home life.

Likewise, a wife should respect her husband's spiritual leadership and work with his leadership in the family and in business. Husbands and wives should be busy doing those things that _build and encourage_ one another.

Our society, our culture, resists both the ideas of authority and submission. American culture prefers anarchy over responsibility, order, servant-authority and submission.

But what our culture prefers does not make God's Word out-dated or wrong. God's Word is the standard that shows _where our culture is wrong._

**Ephesians 5:21 "submitting yourselves to one another . . . in the fear of God."**

- The word fear is the word, "_phobos_"
- "A wholesome dread of displeasing God" (Vine's Expository Dictionary)
- _yearning_ or _strongly desiring_ to please God.
- God's people need to learn to know the Lord well—according to His Word.

This means that as Christian husbands and wives we should fear anything hindering us from _fulfilling_ the responsibilities—the roles—that God gives to each of us in His Word.

166

- God's Word gives directions for Husbands and Wives that help us to order our lives, our homes, our church, and our society.
- Biblical marriages establish a firm foundation for our nation and for our world.

## APPENDIX #4 - GODLY HUSBAND AND GODLY WIFE

**Ephesians 5:25-30    <u>THE GODLY HUSBAND</u>**

The Bible says that marriage is . . . "A great mystery."

- a secret once unknown, now revealed by the Holy Spirit
- (definition of "mystery" as given in Ephesians 3:3-5)

**Ephesians 5:25-30** *Husbands, love your wives, just as Christ also loved the church and gave Himself for her, 26 that He might sanctify and cleanse her with the washing of water by the word, 27 that He might present her to Himself a glorious church, not having spot or wrinkle or any such thing, but that she should be holy and without blemish.*
*28 So husbands ought to love their own wives as their own bodies; he who loves his wife loves himself. 29 For no one ever hated his own flesh, but nourishes and cherishes it, just as the Lord does the church.*
*30 For we are members of His body, of His flesh and of His bones.*

Good marriages have one great primary purpose: TO ILLUSTRATE THE RELATIONSHIP BETWEEN **CHRIST** AND HIS **CHURCH**. The below explanation is taken from the above passage of Scripture, Ephesians 5:25-30.

CHRIST is the pattern for a Godly  HUSBAND

v.25)

- Christ **Loves** the Church. A husband is to **Love** his wife.
- Christ **Gave** Himself for the Church. A husband is to sacrifice himself for his wife if necessary.

- Jesus lived sacrificially and He died for us. A Godly husband dedicates his life and work to his wife and suffers and dies for her if necessary.

v.26)

- Christ **Sanctified** His Church—set Her aside as His own. A husband sees his wife as the only one for him. Just as Jesus comforts and counsels His Church, a Godly husband comforts and counsels his wife.

- Jesus **Cleansed** His Church by His Word. A Godly husband guides his family by God's Word, protecting his wife and children from the dangers of the world.

v. 27)

- Jesus **Presented** His Church to **Himself.** A godly husband presents his family to Christ, trusting the Lord to complete the work in his family.

vs. 28-9)

- Jesus **Nourishes** the Church; He feeds His people and provides our every need. The Lord loves to spend time talking with you (in His Word) and listening to your voice as you talk with Him (in prayer).
- So a Godly husband (as much as he can) **nourishes** and **cherishes** his wife:
    Providing to her:
  Food, shelter, clothing, comfort, joy, confidence
  Time to relax
  Spiritual support
  Shared time

169

Conversation
A trustworthy life
Loving attention
Faithful companionship

When Ephesians 5:29 says, "a husband should love his wife as he *loves himself*," it is saying that a godly husband takes care of himself spiritually, emotionally, and physically, so that he can care for his family.

A Godly husband's role should be as reflexive to care for wife and family as it is for you to protect your face when something comes flying at you.

- Jesus **Cherishes** His Church. The Lord sees His people as precious to Himself—He protects, guards, and honors His people.
- So a Godly husband cherishes his wife, protecting, guarding, and honoring her.

**1 Corinthians 11:3** *But I want you to know that the head of every man is Christ, the head of woman is man, and the head of Christ is God.*

**I Peter 3:1-6** *Wives, likewise, be submissive to your own husbands, that even if some do not obey the word, they, without a word, may be won by the conduct of their wives, 2when they observe your chaste conduct accompanied by fear.*

*3Do not let your adornment be merely outward--arranging the hair, wearing gold, or putting on fine apparel—4rather let it be the hidden person of the heart, with the incorruptible beauty of a gentle and quiet spirit, which is very precious in the sight of God. 5For in this manner, in former times, the holy women who trusted in God also adorned themselves, being submissive to their own husbands, 6as Sarah obeyed Abraham, calling him lord, whose daughters you are if you do good and are not afraid with any terror.*

How can a wife "*be submissive*" (arrange herself) to her husband's leadership?

v.1) For what purpose are wives (esp. of unbelieving husbands)
        to submit to their husband's leadership?
        *that they may win their husbands*

          1.  *Win them* to the Lord.
          2.  *Win* his love.

vs.1-2) Two tools God gives a wife to win her husband:
        v.1) "*without a word*"—that is, by her Christ-like behavior
        v.2) "*chaste conduct*"—faithful in every way to her husband

vs.3-4) Although the woman may be outwardly beautiful, the woman of God is also to display inner beauty.

Inner beauty consists of:
v.4) a. the hidden person of the heart.
b. a gentle and quiet spirit.

vs.5-6) Examples for the woman of God:
Godly women:
a. Trust God
b. Adorn themselves with inner beauty
c. Support and build up their husbands
d. Speak to their husbands with respect


**CONCLUSION:**
Ephesians 5:31-33
v.31) THE TEAM – **Husband** and **Wife**

v.32) THE GREATER TEAM – **Christ** and the
**Church**

v.33) THE COMBINED TEAM – Christ and one
**husband** and one **wife**

**APPENDIX # 5:**

**Some Scriptures on using and saving money.**

### Proverbs 3:9-10
9 Honor the LORD with your possessions, And with the firstfruits of all your increase;
10 So your barns will be filled with plenty, And your vats will overflow with new wine.

### Proverbs 6:6-8
6 Go to the ant, you sluggard! Consider her ways and be wise,
7 Which, having no captain, Overseer or ruler,
8 Provides her supplies in the summer, *And* gathers her food in the harvest.

### Proverbs 13:16
16 Every prudent *man* acts with knowledge, But a fool lays open *his* folly.

### Proverbs 16:2
2 All the ways of a man *are* pure in his own eyes, But the LORD weighs the spirits.

### Proverbs 21:20
20 *There is* desirable treasure, And oil in the dwelling of the wise, But a foolish man squanders it.

### Ecclesiastes 11:2 (TLB)
2 Divide your gifts among many, for in the days ahead you yourself may need much help.

### Joel 2:23-27
23 Be glad then, you children of Zion, And rejoice in the LORD your God; For He has given you the former rain faithfully, And He will cause the rain to come down for you-- The former rain, And the latter rain in the first *month.*
24 The threshing floors shall be full of wheat, And the vats shall overflow with new wine and oil.
25 "So I will restore to you the years that the swarming locust has eaten, The crawling locust, The consuming

locust, And the chewing locust, My great army which I sent among you.

26 You shall eat in plenty and be satisfied, And praise the name of the LORD your God, Who has dealt wondrously with you; And My people shall never be put to shame.

27 Then you shall know that I *am* in the midst of Israel: I *am* the LORD your God And there is no other. My people shall never be put to shame.

### Malachi 3:8-12

8 "Will a man rob God? Yet you have robbed Me! But you say, 'In what way have we robbed You?' In tithes and offerings.

9 You are cursed with a curse, For you have robbed Me, *Even* this whole nation.

10 Bring all the tithes into the storehouse, That there may be food in My house, And try Me now in this," Says the LORD of hosts, "If I will not open for you the windows of heaven And pour out for you *such* blessing That *there will* not *be room* enough *to receive it.*

11 "And I will rebuke the devourer for your sakes, So that he will not destroy the fruit of your ground, Nor shall the vine fail to bear fruit for you in the field," Says the LORD of hosts;

12 "And all nations will call you blessed, For you will be a delightful land," Says the LORD of hosts.

### Matthew 6:25-34

25 "Therefore I say to you, do not worry about your life, what you will eat or what you will drink; nor about your body, what you will put on. Is not life more than food and the body more than clothing?

26 Look at the birds of the air, for they neither sow nor reap nor gather into barns; yet your heavenly Father feeds them. Are you not of more value than they?

27 Which of you by worrying can add one cubit to his stature?

28 So why do you worry about clothing? Consider the lilies of the field, how they grow: they neither toil nor spin;

29 and yet I say to you that even Solomon in all his glory was not arrayed like one of these.

30 Now if God so clothes the grass of the field, which today

is, and tomorrow is thrown into the oven, *will He* not much more *clothe* you, O you of little faith?

31 Therefore do not worry, saying, 'What shall we eat?' or 'What shall we drink?' or 'What shall we wear?'

32 For after all these things the Gentiles seek. For your heavenly Father knows that you need all these things.

33 But seek first the kingdom of God and His righteousness, and all these things shall be added to you.

34 Therefore do not worry about tomorrow, for tomorrow will worry about its own things. Sufficient for the day *is* its own trouble.

### Matthew 25:14-30

14 "For *the kingdom of heaven is* like a man traveling to a far country, *who* called his own servants and delivered his goods to them.

15 And to one he gave five talents, to another two, and to another one, to each according to his own ability; and immediately he went on a journey.

16 Then he who had received the five talents went and traded with them, and made another five talents.

17 And likewise he who *had received* two gained two more also.

18 But he who had received one went and dug in the ground, and hid his lord's money.

19 After a long time the lord of those servants came and settled accounts with them.

20 So he who had received five talents came and brought five other talents, saying, 'Lord, you delivered to me five talents; look, I have gained five more talents besides them.'

21 His lord said to him, 'Well *done,* good and faithful servant; you were faithful over a few things, I will make you ruler over many things. Enter into the joy of your lord.'

22 He also who had received two talents came and said, 'Lord, you delivered to me two talents; look, I have gained two more talents besides them.'

23 His lord said to him, 'Well *done,* good and faithful servant; you have been faithful over a few things, I will make you ruler over many things. Enter into the joy of your lord.'

24 Then he who had received the one talent came and said, 'Lord, I knew you to be a hard man, reaping where you have

not sown, and gathering where you have not scattered seed.
25 And I was afraid, and went and hid your talent in the
ground. Look, *there* you have *what is* yours.'
26 But his lord answered and said to him, 'You wicked and
lazy servant, you knew that I reap where I have not sown,
and gather where I have not scattered seed.
27 So you ought to have deposited my money with the
bankers, and at my coming I would have received back my
own with interest.
28 Therefore take the talent from him, and give *it* to him
who has ten talents.
29 For to everyone who has, more will be given, and he will
have abundance; but from him who does not have, even
what he has will be taken away.
30 And cast the unprofitable servant into the outer
darkness. There will be weeping and gnashing of teeth.'

**1 Timothy 6:17**
17 Command those who are rich in this present age not to
be haughty, nor to trust in uncertain riches but in the living
God, who gives us richly all things to enjoy.

## APPENDIX #6 - GAMBLING AND GOD'S WORD
## (A Bible Study)

This is not a study to prove a point. This is a study for those who love the Lord and believe His Word and desire to know and obey what He has to say about the practice of gambling.

### James 1:25

*But the man who looks intently into the perfect law that gives freedom, and continues to do this, not forgetting what he has heard, but doing it—he will be blessed in what he does.*

**First, gambling is opposed to the principle of faith in God.** We pray for God to provide for our daily needs.

### Matthew 6:11

*Give us today our daily bread.*

### Deut. 8:10-11

*When you have eaten and are satisfied, praise the LORD your God for the good land he has given you. 11Be careful that you do not forget the LORD your God, failing to observe his commands, his laws and his decrees that I am giving you this day.*

**James 1:17**

*Every good and perfect gift is from above, coming down from the Father of the heavenly lights, who does not change like shifting shadows.*

Gambling says to the Lord, "Your gifts are not quite good enough to satisfy me. But that's OK. I can multiply them through gambling."

**Second, gambling gives away the things God has provided** for your family's needs, and to assist others through your generous gifts. If the Lord blesses above your needs, He intends for you to do good with His provision and be generous.

**Proverbs 27:23-27**

*Be sure you know the condition of your flocks, give careful attention to your herds;*

*24for riches do not endure forever, and a crown is not secure for all generations.*

*25When the hay is removed and new growth appears and the grass from the hills is gathered in,*

*26the lambs will provide you with clothing, and the goats with the price of a field.*

*27You will have plenty of goats' milk to feed you and your family and to nourish your servant girls.*

If, like me, you don't have servant girls, this is a promise that God wants to give you a little extra—not to gamble away, but to use for good.

### 1 Tim. 6:17-18 (NIV)

*Command those who are rich in this present world not to be arrogant nor to put their hope in wealth, which is so uncertain, but to put their hope in God, who richly provides us with everything for our enjoyment. [18]Command them to do good, to be rich in good deeds, and to be generous and willing to share.*

**Third, God provides your needs through work** and not through "games." Gambling is not a game, anyway. In a game the rules provide you and your opponent with equal chances to win. Most gambling is biased toward the casino or the dealer.

Essentially gambling is moving money from someone else's pocket to your own (or vice versa). Most cultures call that "stealing," and make it illegal. When it is legalized, it can only be called "legalized stealing."

### Ephes. 4:28

*He who has been stealing must steal no longer, but must **work, doing something useful with his own hands, that he may have something to share with those in need.***

**Genesis 3:19**

*By the sweat of your brow you will eat your food*

*until you return to the ground, since from it you were taken;*

*for dust you are and to dust you will return."*


**1 Corinthians 15:58**

*Therefore, my dear brothers, stand firm. Let nothing move*

*you. Always **give yourselves fully to the work of the***

***Lord**, because you know that your labor in the Lord is not in*

*vain.*


**2 Thessalonians 3:10**

*For even when we were with you, we gave you this rule:*

*"If a man will not work, he shall not eat."*


**Fourth, gambling is idolatry**, God says.


**Isaiah 65:11-12** (NIV)

*"But as for you who **forsake the LORD** and forget my holy*

*mountain,*

*who **spread a table for Fortune** and **fill bowls of mixed***

***wine for Destiny**,*

$^{12}$*I will destine you for the sword, and you will all bend*

*down for the slaughter;*

*for I called but you did not answer, I spoke but you did not*

*listen.*

*You did evil in my sight and chose what displeases me."*

**Fifth, gambling feeds discontent and "the love of money."** God tells us to run from this, and chase after right living.

### 1 Tim. 6:6-11 (NIV)

*But godliness with contentment is great gain. [7]For we brought nothing into the world, and we can take nothing out of it. [8]But **if we have food and clothing, we will be content** with that. [9]People who want to get rich fall into temptation and a trap and into many foolish and harmful desires that plunge men into ruin and destruction. [10]For **the love of money is a root of all kinds of evil. Some people, eager for money, have wandered from the faith** and pierced themselves with many griefs.*

*[11]But you, man of God, **flee from all this, and pursue righteousness**, godliness, faith, love, endurance and gentleness.*

LIFE APPLICATION BIBLE says:

Despite overwhelming evidence to the contrary, most people still believe that money brings happiness. . . . people (who crave) greater riches can be caught in an endless cycle that only ends in ruin and destruction. How can you keep away from the love of money? Paul gives us some guidelines: (1) realize that one day riches will all be gone (1 Tim. 6:7, 17); (2) be content with what you have (1 Tim. 6:8); (3) monitor what you are willing to do to get more money (1 Tim. 6:9-10); (4) love people more than money (1 Tim. 6:11); (5) love God's work more than money (1 Tim. 6:11); (6) freely share what you have with others (1 Tim. 6:18). (See Proverbs 30:7-9 for more on avoiding the love of money.)

**APPENDIX #7 - Enjoying Life Together as a Family** by
Paul and Lois Frederick

## A Scripture Study

**1. Hebrews 10:25** *not forsaking the assembling of
ourselves together, as is the manner of some, but exhorting
one another, and so much the more as you see the Day
approaching.*

    **We need to spend time together.** The expression here,
*"not forsaking the assembling of ourselves together,"* really
was meant for the believers in the congregation to whom
this letter was written. But it can be applied to the family.
Families need to learn to have time together—with each
other—attentive to, and interested in, each other—caring for
each other.

**2. Deuteronomy 6:6-9** *"And these words which I
command you today shall be in your heart. [7] You shall teach
them diligently to your children, and shall talk of them when
you sit in your house, when you walk by the way, when you
lie down, and when you rise up. [8] You shall bind them as a
sign on your hand, and they shall be as frontlets between
your eyes. [9] You shall write them on the doorposts of your
house and on your gates.*

– What was the purpose of all this?
    Likely this was **God's way of preserving faith
among his people and their children.**

**3. So we learn two things:**
    a. We need to spend time together as a family unit
    b. We need to spend time encouraging spiritual growth,
though all activities will not necessarily be spiritual in
nature.

**4. Spending time together creates spiritual growth,**
even if our activities are not always church oriented, Bible
centered, etc.

One Friday evening when our children were young our family had used the old church building for a family activity. We were just leaving when several church girls were arriving. They had seen lights in the church and thought a church activity going on.

"Oh, no," we said. "We were just leaving. This isn't a planned church activity. This is our Family Night."

A little dejected, the girls said, "I wish we had a family night. Our family never does anything together."

**5. How to create one family night every week?** (even couples without children)

    a. Pray about what to do.

    b. Be creative, ask other people what they do, plan, decide what you want to achieve.

    c. You might search your church library for a book on family activities.

**6. Let most things be a surprise. Why?**

    a. Kids, even wives, even husbands (sometime) like a surprise.

    b. If weather changes your plans, the children will have no disappointment because it was a surprise that they never knew about.

    c. Remember that disappointments are remembered longer than fun times.

**7. Families with no children or families with very young infants** do need to spend one entire evening together.

**8. Be flexible.**

Some planning ideas:

1. Develop a Calendar with Family Night events planned for the future.

    - keep the calendar in plain sight

    - if an event has to be canceled, substitute another night or morning for

        a "make-up" family night (morning).

2. Don't try to do too many things at once.

3. Take some goofy pictures now for use later.

184

Plan now to save things in a trunk or old suitcase. Parents might save their children's church drawings and school papers.

Activities that are not expensive:
1. Table games – popcorn
2. Treasure hunt
3. National Geographic night or book night (read to children if they cannot participate in reading yet)
4. Hiking or biking
5. Picnic – at a park where there are slides, swings, etc.
6. Swimming
7. Library and Dairy Queen
8. Special guests
9. Projects – wood, etc.
10. Cookies
11. Picture night
12. Keepsake night – baby clothes, etc.
13. Go to airport to watch planes

Activities – things that might cost something:
1. Museums
2. Tour a downtown city via their skyway
3. Ice show
4. Circus
5. Plays
6. Concerts
7. Visit your state Capital, or an old Cathedral
8. Shopping centers
9. Out to eat
10. Arboretum (plants)
11. Train ride to Duluth

**The Parents' Attitude Toward School** by Paul and Lois Frederick

Pray for:
1. A good and wise teacher for your child
2. A pleasant teacher

Keep open channels of communication for your children to talk with you about their school life.

Take your children to Sunday School classes and Vacation Bible School so they:
1. Become accustomed to being in class away from you.
2. Begin to build spiritual strength and learn proper classroom behavior.

Have a positive attitude about school:
1. Your fear seems to transfer to the child even if you never say anything.
2. Tell fun things you remember about school days.
3. Don't compare your child to the child who can count and read before
    starting kindergarten. By grade 3 or 4, they are all at about the same
    level.
4. Read to your child at a very early age, before they can talk. It's the principle we learn in:

### Deuteronomy 6:6-7

[6] *"And these words which I command you today shall be in your heart.*
[7] *You shall teach them diligently to your children and shall talk of them when you sit in your house, when you walk by the way, when you lie down, and when you rise up.*

Enlist the prayer support of a trusted Christian friend when your child
is going to start school.

Positive attitudes about school.
1. Be very interested in what goes on at school. Attend school functions.

Support your child in school program. Help with school outings.
2. Get to know your child's teacher. Attend PTA – Open Houses – School Conferences.

Let teachers know you pray for them. Invite them (if possible) to your home. Compliment your child's teachers.
3. Assure teachers that you want your child to learn and to get a good education.

Ask what you can do to help your child learn.

Support the teachers. Let them right away know you respect their authority in the classroom.

Try to understand the power of peer pressure.

# BIBLIOGRAPHY

Scriptures taken from the Holy Bible, New International Version®, NIV®. Copyright © 1973, 1978, 1984, 2011 by Biblica, Inc.™ Used by permission of Zondervan. All rights reserved worldwide. www.zondervan.com The "NIV" and "New International Version" are trademarks registered in the United States Patent and Trademark Office by Biblica, Inc.™

Scripture taken from the New King James Version®. Copyright © 1982 by Thomas Nelson. Used by permission. All rights reserved.

Scriptures marked NLT are taken from the HOLY BIBLE, NEW LIVING TRANSLATION (NLT): Scriptures taken from the HOLY BIBLE, NEW LIVING TRANSLATION, Copyright© 1996, 2004, 2007 by Tyndale House Foundation. Used by permission of Tyndale House Publishers, Inc., Carol Stream, Illinois 60188. All rights reserved. Used by permission.

Scriptures marked ESV are taken from the THE HOLY BIBLE, ENGLISH STANDARD VERSION (ESV): Scriptures taken from THE HOLY BIBLE, ENGLISH STANDARD VERSION ® Copyright© 2001 by Crossway, a publishing ministry of Good News Publishers. Used by permission.

Scriptures marked TLB are taken from the THE LIVING BIBLE (TLB): Scripture taken from THE LIVING BIBLE copyright© 1971. Used by permission of Tyndale House Publishers, Inc., Carol Stream, Illinois 60188. All rights reserved.

Life Application Bible: New International Version. Wheaton, IL: Tyndale, 1991. (Life Application Bible, notes)

Vine, W. E., Merrill F. Unger, William White, and W. E. Vine. 1985. Vine's complete expository dictionary of Old and New Testament words. Nashville: Nelson.

Webster, David E., To Love and To Cherish, The C.R. Gibson Company, Norwalk, Connecticut. 1968

Made in the USA
Monee, IL
27 June 2021

71591307R00111